FLOODED F

Floods and the stoical dete
the Fen and Marsh pe
hazardous nature of their work

(1236 – 1947)

TREVOR BEVIS

CROWLAND BRIDGE

ISBN 0 901680 70 2

Published by T. Bevis BA, 28 St. Peter's Road, March, Cambs. PE15 9NA
(Tel: 01354 657286)

Printed by David J. Richards, Printers and Stationers, 1 West Park Street,
Chatteris, Cambs. PE16 6AH
(Tel: 01354 692947)   (Fax: 01354 692299)

Many church towers in the Marshland, like that at West Walton, became places of refuge in times of flood.

FLOODED FENS

Introduction

Documents exist telling of "the rage of the sea" and how it affected Wisbech and several nearby villages. In 1250 the town, virtually surrounded with water, had several valuable messuages which were utterly destroyed by the "rage". Wisbech developed on a system of flood defences consisting of embankments and it was perilously near the flood plain which was frequently inundated by the sea and by freshwater. Between 1250 and 1350 the marshland between King's Lynn and Wisbech was flooded to great depths on no less than twelve occasions. Matthew Paris recorded in his *Chronica Majora* instances of great damage inflicted on Marshland. A devastating flood occurred in 1338 and this and others occurring before that year, instigated alarm and the matter was reviewed by a jury at Wiggenhall.

The incidents were worrying and threatened the whole of the area with total submersion. The precariousness of Wisbech and its attendant villages was known for a long time and the chronicler penned "On the morrow after Epiphany in the third year of the King, a certain bank on the west side of the river (Ouse) by means of the raging sea, broke; so that the tide entered and overflowed a thousand acres of land, some with corn, to the great damage of the same town. And that on the west part of the said river, by reason of the like tempests . . . the before specified bank was broken and torn, so that the tide entered, bore down a house and overflowed acres of land sown with corn. And that . . . the same bank by like mishap, broken again for the length of three furlongs in a certain place called Barty's Hythe, insomuch as the tides flowing in overwhelmed the land".

It was much the same story at Walpole, West Walton, Walsoken, Tilney, Emneth and Terrington where similar inundations occurred only too frequently. Acres of arable land and domestic premises "were drowned and utterly lost for ever by the inundation of the sea". The people of Marshland lived in terror of "the outrageousness of the sea," beset by fearful tempests and unrelenting violence of the tide which brought about "sudden inundation and violence, as well of the sea as of the fresh water". At the same time the coastal area of South Lincolnshire suffered severe losses due to tidal surge. The inhabitants of these places bitterly complained about loss of goods,

I

land and crops and the townships (known as villages nowadays) received help in that taxes were remitted in part. In 1336 the householders of Emneth, Walsoken and West Walton petitioned for allowance in respect of severe losses and were given a rebate of "eight out of sixty pounds". In 1342 taxes raised by Tydd and Newton, near Wisbech, were much lower because of the seriousness of tidal inundation which had drowned the land and ruined growing crops.

In 1423 at Long Sutton complaints were made that the land was often overflown with great amounts of water and rendered unusable for a considerable time. The town was almost surrounded with sea water and the inhabitants were obliged to row in boats over the sodden land. They were charged for every acre more than thirty pence, this causing ruination to most. The inhabitants blamed their misfortune on their neighbours at Whaplode, Gedney and Holbeach who apparently failed to maintain the "sewers" (dykes and drains).

Appointed commissions had conservation of the Fens at heart and their duty involved surveying the areas relating to their responsibility, and to reform and compel those whose duty it was to maintain sea defences. Every landowner "according to the proportion of his tenure, repair, maintain and new make" dykes and drains as often as necessary. The sea banks also fell under their scrutiny and the men of the Walton villages were fully responsible for their sections of the protective embankment. In 1348 at West Walton the townspeople "did yearly repair for every acre of .land lying in the said town, six feet and two inches of the sea banks". Also for every acre they had to maintain one foot of the Pokediche bank. A similar arrangement affected the men of Walsoken.

In some places, for instance at Elm and Welle (Outwell) where flooding was not as pronounced, for every acre a man owned he paid twopence and more should it be necessary, this termed as "agistments" in efforts to impede the flow of a certain stream which was causing damage to the land, and they also had to make good a causeway.

For a long time before the 16th century, despite regularity of flooding, the fens and marsh areas were notable as being highly productive. In the 13th century there existed large acreages of arable land drained by ditches which separated the fields. Even in the 11th century at Deeping Richard de Rulos raised embankments and "from sloughs and bogs made a pleasure garden"

Matthew Paris, 13th century historian, wrote: "Concerning this marsh a wonder has happened in our time. For in years past, beyond living memory, these places were accessible for neither man nor beast, with only deep mud and sedge and reeds, and inhabited by birds, indeed more likely by devils as appears from the life of St. Guthlac who began to live there and found it a place of horror and solitude. This is now changed into delightful meadows and also arable grounds. What therefore does not produce corn or hay brings forth abundant sedge, turf and other fuel which is very useful to the inhabitants of the region".

Fen islands elevated above the peat levels were well cultivated and had the advantage of remaining free of floods. Chroniclers were generous in their praise of places such as Ely "the fairest place" and "the most beautiful vill of Ramsey". Crowland and Thorney were each beheld as a paradise producing vines and fruit in great abundance. "Ramsey the Golden" was virtually surrounded by meres and marsh and enjoyed the presence of a great Benedictine abbey luring pilgrims from all over the country. It was regarded in England and abroad as one of the highest schools of learning.

It was written: "In length, the island (of Ramsey) extends two miles, but is not as wide, being surrounded with alders, reeds, green canes and bullrushes which beautify it exceedingly. Before it became inhabited it was full of all kinds of trees, the size of which may be seen from the beams and rafters in the roof of the church. But through the space of time the woods have almost disappeared and the fertility of the turf is such that the tilled land bears corn plentifully; nor is it less profitable otherwise, being full of fair gardens, rich pastures, sturdy groves and rich meadows which in springtime look most beautiful". This description belies the usual statements that the Fen air was obnoxious and perpetually charged with mists.

Hay was one of the main crops in the Fens of old and large expanses of pasture existed for grazing animals. According to the season water levels fluctuated and in the dry season this resulted in areas very suitable for pasturage. Meadow land was more valuable than tilled land and marshland proper was of very low value. Fen pasture was of higher value than that on the upland and propositions to drain it were unwelcome, winter inundation actually enriching it. Turves were plentiful and were dried out in areas excluded to cattle for fear of animals damaging them. Only stipulated areas of fen were earmarked for turf digging which was carried out at appropriate times of the year in accordance with the regulations. There existed the right "to cut, to dig, to burn, or to pare at all times at will and to give or to sell". This right dated to earliest times. People living on the upland areas were unable to purchase fen turf and the fen commoners held the right to use it for fuel.

Centuries ago land in the north of Cambridgeshire was highly valuable to farmers. It generally comprised a mixture of peat and silt introduced by sea incursion and sometimes freshwater pouring into the Fens from the upland. Silt land proper extended from the peat edge to the coast and was even more valuable to owners. It generated a great deal of wealth which can be seen in the opulence of fine parish churches, many dating to the 15th and 16th centuries or being completely restored and embellished during those times. Surprisingly, the silt supports huge churches first built in the 12th century and given magnificent aisles, naves and chancels, noble towers and spires as will be seen at Tilney All Saints and Walsoken (Norman), West Walton and Tydd St. Giles (Early English), Terrington St. Clement (a huge church more like a 14th century priory with more than eighty windows), and that unspoilt perpendicular masterpiece at Walpole St. Peter.

Other great churches indicative of medieval marsh farmers' status are those at Moulton, Whaplode, Holbeach, Pinchbeck, Spalding, Gedney and Donnington built on the strength of wheat, cheese, sheep, cattle, dairies and geese. All this derived from back-breaking work in a highly dangerous environment where the farmer had to be prepared to lose everything to the rage of the sea; to adapt himself to the life of a fisherman and be a drainage engineer at the same time and build and maintain embankments. He had also to be expert at predicting the weather which brought him a mixture of good fortune and bad. He was marshman and fenman and his persistence in the face of everything that nature could throw at him brought him rich dividends.

FLOODS AT MURROW BANK

Many times I wandered seated upon a cycle saddle along the length of Murrow Bank which is what I usually call it, defined in the stretch of slightly elevated road of about five miles between Guyhirn and Parson Drove. In olden times it was referred to as Fen Dyke. This ridge of raised earth is nowhere as high as it used to be and it follows the trend of several embankments in the Fens thrown up to protect virile, highly productive reclaimed land against the onrush of freshwater and salt water floods. Murrow Bank carries the road above the former flood plain as do other ancient embankments in the Fens such as those at Leverington and between Newton and the Tydd villages. The so called Roman Banks in particular formed a protective barrier for the townships against sea water incursion and they played a vital, though not always successful role in the protection of these low lying areas of valuable reclaimed land.

Murrow Bank links three villages, namely Guyhirn, Murrow and Parson Drove. The bank road has always been the direct means of communicating with these villages and gives access to Wisbech, March and Peterborough. Several minor roads exist in the vicinity allowing access to nearby places but centuries ago the fen causeways were usually under water in winter and only during clement weather conditions were people able to travel in reasonable safety to Wisbech St. Mary, Leverington and Newton and also Gedney and Crowland accessible by using the embankment road from Clough's Cross near Parson Drove. Murrow Bank was vitally important to nearby parishes in medieval times and not only protected the inhabitants from floods but allowed relatively safe travel and, more importantly from the aspect of the local economy, for most part it protected the east side comprised of virile land in the vicinity of Wisbech St. Mary and Leverington from the threat of fresh water flooding from the direction of Wryde.

It is thought that Murrow Bank was thrown up during the 14th century by Wisbech's prolific Holy Trinity Guild, a semi-religious corporate organisation which undertook to build and maintain earth embankments in the area. The guild was familiar with the consequences of disastrous flooding on a colossal scale and made prodigious efforts to maintain the embankment between Guyhirn and Clough's Cross, effectively dividing the east and west fens, leaving that on the west (Wryde) side more or less to chance and saving, hopefully, the more prolific fen on the east side towards Wisbech. In medieval times the vast acreage of marsh in the direction of

1

Wryde was, for best part of the year, a morass. From the 17th century to the mid-18th century it was only sporadically farmed, depending on weather conditions. One of the main crops grown near Thorney was a wild cabbage, quite inedible, known as colza much favoured by the Huguenot and Walloon colonists that settled in the area from 1646 onwards. The crop, like sedge, grew prolifically in these parts and was valued for its oil which was particularly good for the softening of wool as well as providing fuel for lamps. West of Murrow Bank the fen produced an abundance of sedge and reeds. During the winter season parishioners from the three villages descended upon the fen with scythes to harvest the crop. Quite often the water was frozen and sledges and dog carts ladened with sedge and reeds were dragged to local barns to await transportation to upland areas.

In winter villagers could do little on cultivated fields east of the embankment, seasonal work temporarily halted by weather conditions. The work on the sedge and reed beds helped in no small measure to sustain the local economy. Casting our eyes over the cultivated land nowadays belies the original conditions. It is all taken for granted. Two-hundred-and-fifty years ago the aspect was totally different and work was fraught with danger at every turn. The Fens claimed many victims, some falling from boats and drowning; others sinking into the mire and suffocating. When fog began to descend at dusk as it often did should anyone working in the marsh ignore the bells chiming from church towers and delaying their departure it might well be too late and they became disorientated. It was recorded in the 19th century that the marsh had given up its dead here and there, some bodies covered by layers of silt and peat for hundreds of years, emerging into the light after four or five centuries, almost perfectly preserved. Peat in particular has a remarkable preservative effect and human bodies retrieved from silt near Spalding in the 19th century were found to be near perfect.

Murrow Bank had to be regularly inspected for signs of weakness and repairs had to be carried out frequently. Hundreds of years ago local men living in the vicinity of the embankment were on emergency standby throughout the winter when water up to depths of six feet lay heavily against the west wall of the barrier. Submersion of the fen between Wryde and the embankment depended on the amount of water passing beneath Wansford bridge near Peterborough. That the men of Murrow, Guyhirn and Parson Drove were so fastidious with the well-being of the embankment was, of course, entirely in their own interests. Probably the Guild of the Holy Trinity insisted on proper maintainance.

2

Despite efforts to keep the water at bay serious breaches did occur and the usual manner of dealing with this was to rebuild the affected part, usually after the gushing water had subsided. The repaired section was built outwards similar to a fortress bastion. This was a half moon wedge protruding on the west side, the curve reinforced with lengths of wickerwork. In my earlier days I was puzzled at the odd bends in the road which made no sense at all, since the rest of the road was almost perfectly straight. In recent years a new piece of road was made across one of the bends, but the other, the site of a torrent of angry water, remains. The significance of these bends is that they mark the site of major breaches which occurred at the bank centuries ago. Millions of gallons of water poured through the gaps and water spread out on the east side engulfing everything it came up against in the vicinity of Tholomas Drove, Wisbech St. Mary, Murrow, Leverington and Parson Drove.

Breaches began modestly in obviously weaker parts of the embankment and as the water built up and gained weight they became wider, as much as one or two hundred yards. Once started nothing could be done to stop the inflow and only when million of tonnes had passed through the gaps and equalised the level on the east side was it possible to plug the gap. These two events were the most serious to affect the area and as a result the local economy lay in ruins for at least two years. Numerous unrecorded breaches before the 15th century probably occurred. In winter the embankment was frequently patrolled as were most others in the Fens and should any fissure be discovered it was promptly dealt with, gangs of men working night and day if necessary to repair and strengthen the bank.

A local man, Thomas Flowers, entrusted with land and responsible for the operation of a sluice in the bank was blamed for one of the floods. The sluice controlled inflow of water from the Fen Dyke hard against the embankment, this used for irrigation purposes. Cultivated strips of land abounded between Wisbech St. Mary and Murrow and in normal times the Dyke proved very useful to the farmers. One day when water was beginning to build up to the west of the embankment, Mr. Flowers went to sleep. Waking up, to his consternation he discovered the water was pouring through with such strength it was impossible to close the sluice gate. The sluice fell apart and the outlet became host to a raging torrent which clawed out a huge gap in the

Bank. Water covered the holdings by as much as six feet in depth and thousands of acres were rendered useless for at least two years. What happened to Mr. Flowers nobody knows!

Murrow, Parson Drove and Guyhirn survived against the odds, the villages sometimes inundated with spillage from the River Welland far to the west. It was much the same story at Terrington St. Clement, the community tragically overcome by the sea which breached the barrier. Inhabitants had to rely on genius and experience when their homes were invaded by the brine. When disaster struck, usually without warning, people collected what belongings they could carry and sought refuge in the church tower until waters subsided. In the 17th century several families resorted to the "flood tower" and were sustained by the people of King's Lynn using boats to carry blankets and victuals. It's remarkable how Fen parishes emerged from similar disasters. Stoical determinedness was the key. Fen people were not lacking in that way. Hardness of life can bring out the better qualities and, of course, is can also break a person's resolve. Acceptance of nature's unremitting ways is the hallmark of true Fen people who learned to face the odds with admirable determination and somehow they won through time and time again. Hope springs eternal but on occasions tragedy struck . . . a whole community swept away, lives lost, stock drowned, habitations destroyed, anguished survivors having to start all over again.

In the 13th century it was written that a village near Wisbech, thought to be Newton, succumbed to the terrible rage of the sea which breached the embankments. Almost a hundred inhabitants were drowned and all that remained intact were the ruins of a chapel. Wisbech, too, received horrific visitations of a similar nature, being severely flooded in about 1236 and experiencing loss of life and property. The castle suffered great damage and had to be rebuilt. All Marshland villages were occasionally inundated by the sea or fresh water. A tablet inside West Walton church tells of those calamities in poignant manner. Why did people persist in putting up with vengeful forays of water when they could have moved to higher ground? Simply because they related to marsh and fen, their allotted space in life. Fair weather or foul the Fen people never accepted defeat.

It is clear that a few minor marsh settlements were utterly destroyed by floods, the sea in angry mood forcing a passage into reclaimed ground. This happened between Terrington St. Clement and Long Sutton, and where the Wash narrowed near Wisbech an inflow is known to have overcome a small

4

hamlet in the region of Tydd St. Giles. The flooding of Marshland makes fascinating study, and it was due to its enterprising and determined inhabitants that laboriously eked out a living of sorts as well as maintained the sea bank that any vestige of order existed at all. The water gate at Clough's Cross and the infamous four "Gotes" at Tydd introduced a measure of normality in the battle against the sea. The Gotes were timber sluice gates fairly close together which were supposed to act as safety valves and protect the Tydd villages and the area extending to Parson Drove and Newton from tidal surge. The district was notorious for periodic inflows of water urged on by high winds and the equally notorious Aegar, a combination of easterly gales which forced incoming tides to pulverise the embankments and exploited their weaknesses. The situation was at its worst when the tides began to turn and wanted to go nowhere in particular, being forced by gales to climb the embankments. Then it was a disaster in the making. Not only did the water run over the top it often caused the earth barriers to collapse and Wisbech and villages nearby were completely engulfed. In recent years medieval drainage pipes were discovered in the Roman Bank between Leverington and Tydd St. Giles which implies that measures were taken to drain off the flooded level when it was practicable to do so.

Returning to Murrow Bank, I sometimes stop at the Gull, the surviving bend in the road, and try to imagine the scenes of frenzied activity following a breach along the bank. Every fit man living in the vicinity joined forces in an attempt to stem the flow and repair the gap. At Thorney a system was devised to warn the village and outlying farms of pending disaster. In exceptionally rainy seasons men placed long stakes at equal distances along the water's edge, an inch or two protruding above the surface. Small groups patrolled the banks and were careful to observe the rising water, particularly the stakes. If water covered the top of the stakes apparently all was well, but if it had dropped against the markers the observers knew that somewhere along the bank a breach had occurred and water was pouring onto the land. Mounted men standing by hurriedly galloped to the village and outlying farms and warned the people who carried possessions into upper chambers.

Having examined the meaning of "gote", what does the place-name Murrow mean? It smacks of the marsh. "Mur-" contains a Celtic root and in almost every place where it occurs, as in the North Country and in Ireland it relates to water, a beach or marsh. Murrow was aptly named. In days of yore it was very much a watery place, the embankment rising above the little community, with sedge grounds and flood plains far to the west and when

5

In medieval times earth embankments were the most
important precaution against sea and fresh water inundation.
They still are. Embankments were vital in the protection of reclaimed
areas in the coastal region and the Fen interior. Earth barriers
were susceptible to severe damage by "the rage of the sea"
and by excessive amounts of fresh water building up against
them in inland areas. Fenmen resident in adjacent villages
regularly inspected the banks and made repairs.

The illustration shows the medieval sea bank near Newton.

(Photo: LILIAN REAM
with permission of THE LILIAN REAM COLLECTION)

not under cultivation the land eastwards, some of it marsh, was in peril of being flooded from the Roman Bank near Newton or from a collapsed section of the earthwork nearby. As a Fenman might say: "You takes your pick and choose salt water or fresh!" In ancient language "-row" indicates the existence of several dwelling places, in those days crude little cottages or huts. Murrow, then, means "a row of cottages by the marsh".

Alas, Murrow has no claim to fame. But wait a minute! I'm not so sure. Years ago I was puzzled by an oddness in that there were two sets of railway lines crossing each other. One, the LNER line from March to York, the other the MGN dubbed by grandfather Bevis, a signalman at Murrow, the "muddle-and-get-nowhere line" running from the heart of Norfolk to Peterborough. There were only two such arrangements in the country. So yes! Murrow was in fact distinguished by this rare rail phenomenon. No thanks to Mr. Beeching, all this, like the original row of cottages beside the marsh dissipated into the mists of time. A large broken-down concrete signalbox occupies the site of the old traditional wooden structure where my bearded grandfather worked. He lived in a cottage in Mill Lane and he liked to show me a pet toad which lived in a cold frame and was regularly fed by him. It was unusual that a little place like Murrow possessed a couple of signalboxes, the other worked by my uncle, Charlie Hart. My family was steeped in railway tradition. A very enthusiastic railway guard, my father, Fred was born in the cottage and married Elsie May Allen, daughter of David Allen, farmer along Hooks Drove. On their marriage at Murrow Methodist chapel my parents moved to Pinchbeck where I was born and when ten years of age I moved with my parents to March. From this, readers will deduce that part of my roots are at Murrow and the same can be said of Parson Drove and Guyhirn. This, indeed, is the land of my fathers.

By all accounts Murrow is an old place but has little to show for it. The Anglican church derives from Corpus Christie, an earlier building, which dated at least to the 14th century and in all probability stood on the site occupied by the existing church. The original church was like the ancient fen chapels, in this case under the jurisdiction of the priest at Wisbech St. Mary, much as St. John the Baptist church, Parson Drove was administered for a time by the priest at Leverington. Some of these fen chapels were little gems in an architectural sense but were left to decay after the Dissolution and were not replaced until much later in the 19th century when alterations to ecclesiastical boundaries took place and in some cases small, adequate churches built on the site of a previous ancient building.

An idea of the hazardous times experienced by the bank people comparatively recently is recalled in a story which originated in the 19th century. A Murrow resident died and, according to the usual practice, the service and burial arranged to take place at St. John the Baptist church, Parson Drove. The church is not more than two miles from Murrow. Usually traffic and funerals went from village to village via Murrow Bank but in winter the road was transformed into a quagmire and riddled with potholes. The undertaker wanted to take the horse and cart conveying the coffin and immediate mourners to the church across the fields which he considered was a better proposition than risking the journey by road. However, the feoffees controlling the land between the two villages refused his request on the grounds that a precedent would be set and so the sad little procession had no choice but use the road which in normal conditions was right and proper. The road had deep ruts and water had filled the potholes. It was, in fact, far worse than the fields. By all accounts the corpse and the mourners had a most uncomfortable journey and it took four hours to arrive at the church. The bereaved then had the gruelling task of going home the same way by the same means and the journey took just as long.

As far as place-names go Parson Drove is self-explanatory. The village, probably founded in the 13th century, developed along a very long drove and was served by a priest at Leverington. Priests had the daunting task of negotiating dangerous droves awash with water in order to administer to their flocks in far-flung places. To minimise the risks, whenever possible, the inhabitants of Parson Drove had to travel, especially on festive days, to Leverington. This was not uncommon practice. Parson Drove may have originated from Fitton End, the chapel there having become so ruinous the congregation obliged to attend services at Parson Drove where a new chapel had been built. There were several small chapels in the Fens and in medieval times they were reasonably maintained. While most fell to ruin during the Reformation a few were elevated to the status of church to serve a defined ecclesiastical parish. St. John's was one, a chapel at first, then a church and now sadly redundant.

A redundant church signifies failure for all sorts of reasons, mainly lack of interest by people. A lot of money is spent on them by preservation societies which to some people is a good thing worthy of our splendid heritage, and others regard it as a waste of money as the buildings, by law, can no longer be regularly used. A church becomes redundant for the want of a congregation and the parish share impossible to raise. Realistically, in some places in the future many of these "neglected" churches will become unsustainable and be allowed to crumble into the ground. It appears that Parson Drove's Old Church was rebuilt in the early 15th century. I say rebuilt as in its shallow north porch is a doorway dating back to the 13th century. Before the Victorian church was built at Southea, a part of Parson Drove, the Old Church was the centre of village activities. It followed the trend after the Black Death in the building of new churches on the site of old ones. They were refashioned after the ideal of practical buildings lending themselves to community use and, of course, for the traditional services. For instance, in the event of bumper harvests and tithe barns were filled to bursting, the churches were used for the storage of grain. In Georgian and Victorian times the church buildings lost much of their practical value and were used solely for Sunday services and christenings, weddings and funerals. For several years during the early 18th century St. John the Baptist church was used by a colony of Huguenots and Walloons who were allowed to hold their services in the French tongue. These were conducted by the Reverend Henry Pujolas who was unfamiliar with English and the native congregation drifted away.

Several Huguenot families are buried in the churchyard with their minister. Most of the foreign names became Anglicised and married into local families. Henry Pujalos was sent to this outpost in the Fens for some mild misdeed, the usual reason for having the audacity to challenge the French colloque. The English wardens paid him a meagre salary and later it was discovered "that the wardens who farmed the church land, deducted part of the poor man's wages and kept it for themselves". This eventually led to an ecclesiastical inquiry. I treasure happy memories of times in these parts before and during the Second World War. It was on the family farm along Hook's Drove, Murrow, where I was set free from the detested ritual of attending Pinchbeck Primary school. David Allen, maternal grandfather farmed land in the vicinity and I recall one hot balmy day on the Twenty Acre field, sitting in a bone dry ditch with him and uncle Wilfred, eating cheese and pickled onion sandwiches, topped up with a grenadier apple and a flask of tea to wash it all down. Believe me, that was really living!

THE CORNER OF THE SALT WATER DITCH

This heading refers to the meaning of Guyhirn's name. My family's link with the flood plains of old extends to the village, a one-sided place dwarfed by the substantial banks of the tidal River Nene. The Culy's on my mother's side lived here and they can be traced as far back as the 16th century at least, the English line having its origin at Brussels. There Henry Culy supplied fine cloth to the nobility until the Church of Rome forbade him, he being an avid Protestant, a dangerous thing to be on the Continent in those distant times. He and his wife, Joice, a linen packer, pulled up their roots and along with countless others sought religious freedom in England.

The restless Nene flows back and forth and the traffic it carried a couple of hundred years ago is no more. All is very quiet now. The old cart bridge has gone and a new one replaces it carrying the much maligned and over-used main road from the Midlands to East Anglia. The new bridge more or less isolated Guyhirn, pushing it aside so to speak, and access is hardly any better than that to Parson Drove and Murrow.

Two bishops were familiar with Guyhirn, one a proper bishop, the other a self-styled bishop who lost no love on the Anglican church. The feeling was mutual. The former mentioned prelate ought to have been a qualified drainage engineer. When not involved with Church matters he dabbled with experimental land drainage and entertained the idea of ridding the fens between Guyhirn and Stanground of excessive amounts of water. Bishop Morton of Ely, later Archbishop of Canterbury and Cardinal of all England, envisaged the flood plain as potentially prosperous ground for Wisbech and Whittlesey farmers. In about 1486 he designed a new leam, appropriately named after him and which continues to do good service within the general design of the Fens' drainage scheme. The leam attaches itself to the River Nene at Guyhirn at a point near Ring's End where the enterprising bishop built a stone tower to observe the lineage of his creation. On occasions he ascended the tower with measuring instruments to ascertain that the leam was progressing favourably and to determine the depth and width as far as the horizon allowed. Bishop Morton, brimful with ideas caused a large lagoon to be excavated near the leam and "Wisbech River". At appropriate times water from the leam filled the lagoon and when the tide had turned, the basin discharged its water at great force into the river, scouring its bed all the way to Wisbech, displacing the silt and carrying it into the Wash. Well, that was the theory but it did not always work.

9

The bishop's commendable idea failed on a few unconsidered points. He had the leam excavated insufficiently wide enough nor deep enough. It did indeed collect water but in winter, there being no high banks, it was inclined to discharge into the marsh and floods occurred as far away as the old course of the Nene between Benwick and March. Farmers working in the pastures alongside the leam and at Whittlesey did not help matters and took advantage of the shallow depth, dropping gravel and stones onto the leam's bed by which convenience they might cross to the other side. One day I discovered several large stone slabs beneath the turf close to where the leam joined the River Nene. It occurred to me that these probably formed the base of the observation tower used by the bishop and his surveyors. Bishop Morton was a remarkably talented man. It is not generally known that he was the principal mediator in restoring peace between the warring Houses of Lancaster and York. When he died, a witness at his bedside recorded " . . . and so this energetic man passed away, unto the very end his head filled with astonishing powers".

From the observation tower the bishop must have often looked at the cottages on the opposite side of the river. The small, beautiful "gem of a chapel" built in the 13th century like a spiritual oasis in this watery place came to his view. Its site is occupied by the existing Victorian church. The Dissolution of the Monasteries in which Henry VIII declared his intention "not to destroy but reform", had the opposite effect. The spectre of centralisation of which we in our own day and age have more than enough, spilled over from the wanton destruction of beautiful monasteries which had succoured countryside traditions. The change affected numerous little chapels including those which were to be found at Throckenholt, Eldernell, Murrow, Newton and indeed, Guyhirn and they were left to decay or the stones used to build barns and cottages. The Reformed Church raised its standard over all England accompanied by a sense or apprehension accentuated by the demise of guilds, and embraced every man, woman and child, perhaps more so in the Fens where monasteries had been ten-a-penny. Reorganisation of parochial boundaries repaired some of the damage and curates and vicars were inducted at newly built churches built on the sites of ancient edifices as was evidenced at Murrow and Guyhirn.

From about 1650 individuals and small groups began turning away from established Church practice and founded different Christian groups. The Baptists and Quakers came into being, followed by Methodists and Independents. John Wesley broke away from the Anglican Church and preached to congregations assembled in graveyards. Wesleyan chapels sprang up all over the country and the Anglican Church itself split, if that's the appropriate word, into two categories termed high and low.

Independent churches appeared and various religious sects, too. At Guyhirn a Walloon family played its part in local religious activities. It was known as the Culimite assembly and, in its heyday, enjoyed a following in the former Isle of Ely of about nine hundred souls scattered in the Fens at Needingworth, Isleham, Upwell, March, Wisbech and, of course, Guyhirn. The Culy family can be traced to Hatfield Chase, near Doncaster, Norwich, London , Dover and across the sea to Brussels where, in about 1560, Henry and John Culy supplied fine cloth to the nobility. The Culy's were avid Protestants, then a dangerous thing in the Holy Roman empire. Many persecuted Protestant families, including the Culy's, fled in some cases literally for their lives to Protestant England. Their children were born in England and the generations moved around East Anglia settling notably at Norwich, where one became an Alderman and later Mayor in recognition of his services in restoring peace between the English and Flemish weaving fraternities.

One of the family joined several others who trekked to Hatfield Chase where Cornelius Vermuyden, the Dutch land drainage engineer, had drawn up a scheme to drain an area of fen. The English, however, had other ideas and did everything imaginable to deter the Walloons and Huguenots from the task, burning their houses, breaking embankments and sluices and creating mayhem. After twelve years the families had had enough and they, with the Culy's, came to Thorney to help Vermuyden with the drainage scheme in the Isle of Ely. The Culy's settled at Guyhirn and there David Culy founded the Culimite sect. The Bishop of Ely, embittered over David's preaching, attempted to have him pressed into the navy at King's Lynn. The hard boiled sailors discovered that Culy had a secret weapon, namely his voice, and he fervently sang hymns, most of which he himself had written, and they earnestly implored the captain to put him ashore off Yarmouth. When safely ashore David made his way back to Guyhirn, preaching on the way, and his friends made him a landowner at Ring's End which ascertained he could never be deported.

David Culy went to his task with even greater determination and with the Bishop of Ely in mind actually founded a church at Isleham in the bishop's backgarden, so to speak! He also founded a church at Billinghay in Lincolnshire. Culy visited Christ Church Baptist congregation at March in 1690 and one ponders as to why he did not join. The minister, Pastor Holcroft, had formed a congregation at Guyhirn a few years previously but it seems to have fallen away and Culy, a natural leader one supposes, recognised the opportunity to establish a religious base at the village. He visited Cambridge for advice and wrote: "I had great desires to be in some church but not that (at Cambridge). But yet I know no other but a Baptiz church and that I could not joyne withal".

In February 1691 Pastor Richard Davis, a well-known preacher, visited Guyhirn. He was based from 1689 to 1714 at the Independent Church at Rothwell in Northamptonshire (Culy called it "Rowell"). Davis was zealous for the spread of the Gospels and his tireless zeal won numerous converts throughout that county and neighbouring shires. His spirited presentation was just the tonic Culy needed. "To him the Lord knit my heart to immediately".

Thus the ground was prepared for firm growth in religious matters at Guyhirn. In the same year Culy with five villagers – four men and two women - set off for distant Rothwell and were received into the fellowship. Through this simple act of faith the fellowship at Guyhirn became a branch of the Rothwell Church and David Culy made an Elder. From time to time Pastor Davis visited the fledgling Church and during the following months an encouraging number of converts joined. Many were former members of the Anglican Church and the new-found congregation became known as The Culimites. By the summer of 1693 Culy had become well known throughout the Isle of Ely and in parts of southern Cambridgeshire. Some members were resident at Soham, Needingworth, Outwell, Denver, Newmarket, Thetford, Southery, March and Elm.

It was not long before Culy began exploring ways and means of detaching Guyhirn's fellowship from Rothwell and becoming a separate Church. Eventually a letter of "dismission" was sent to The Church In The Fens and on July 26th 1693 at Rothwell in the presence of several pastors and messengers from far and near Culy and his fellowship received the blessing of all present and the Guyhirn Church became an independent one. Culy was duly recognised as pastor on November 11th of the same year. At the inception of the Church the membership comprised forty souls, twenty-two brethren and eighteen sisters. The writer possesses the names of each one and the places where they lived.

David Culy extended his "parish" very successfully and was uncompromising in doctrinal approach. Overburdened with independence and driven by conviction he often placed himself, one is inclined to think deliberately, in antagonistic situations with the Anglican Church and his zeal for verbal confrontation seems to have gone a little too far at times. Later his opinions enmeshed his own followers and sadly, even his friend Richard Davis fell out with him. The break transpired from Culy's "errors and unsound expressions" observed in 1695 but it was not until 1702 that the Rothwell fellowship issued a testimony against him and his adherants.

When he set up the fellowship at Billinghay, not surprisingly he found himself at odds with the local vicar. In "The Works Of David Culy" there is recorded the expected confrontation with the Reverend Blaxley in 1719 "when the reverend gentleman did challenge Mr. David Culy to dispute with him on such a day at the cross openly". Culy, who was no newcomer to verbal dispute, turned up with most of the townspeople but there was no sign of the vicar. After some considerable time had elapsed, Mr. Blaxley appeared but declined to dispute and instead thrust a letter into Culy's hand outlining the charges against him. In "The Works, etc." Culy warmly defends himself against the vicar's insinuations. David Culy undoubtedly enjoyed strong popularity in Lincolnshire, this confirmed in a letter published in Fenland Notes And Queries. From this we learn that "the Culimites were well known in Lincolnshire and must have been at one time very numerous there, since even in the present day (circa 1900) the name is frequently applied to all dissenters".

David Culy's energies were not entirely confined to the pulpit and wayside exhortation. An equally natural outlet was that of his versatile pen. That Culy could read and write when so many at that time could not, was an advantage in more ways than one. This, coupled with his gift of elocution made him a leader. He loved books and, himself an author, he made time to study great works by others. The Word of Life was ever with him and infused him with strength for the morrow, come what may. Indeed, there were times when he had particular need of it.

Culy wrote numerous hymns. Perusing them lends the impression that when devoted to his work in quiet surroundings he rose to full spiritual stature. Seventeenth century hymnology is a subject not too well documented and Culy's contribution is worthy of more detailed study. The structure of his verse in common with most other hymn writers of his time is, of course, much different to the style and inspirational qualities seen in our own age. The hymns are recorded in a hand-written volume kept in the Wisbech and Fenland Museum. The first page is an introduction, thus: "Hymns on diverse subjects by David Culy, preacher of the Gospel at Guyhorn near Wisbech in the Isle of Ely and County of Cambridge and was compos'd in the year of Our Lord One Thousand Six Hundred and Ninety Two, Three and Four. (Coppy'd out of Isaac Culy's Book written by John Creasey) by John Culy of Guyhorn aforesaid August the 13th Ann Christi 1771".

"The Works Of David Culy" first appeared as a joint edition with "The Glory Of The Two Crowned Heads, Adam And Christ Unveiled" by the same author (London 1726). This volume was reprinted at Boston in 1787 and anther edition appeared separately at Plymouth Dock in 1800 and later at Spilsby in 1820. "The Works, etc." also included a section headed: "Letters And Answers To And From Various Ministers Of Diverse Persuasions On Various Subjects", together with "Above Forty Hymns Compos'd On Weighty Subjects ".

At its inception the Culimites met in unlicensed houses and it was not until September 28th 1751 that Hugh Foster, minister, Isaac Culy and Peter Delahoi, elders, together with Isaac Melton, Ammi Culy, John Scouler and Manasshah Culy applied for licenses to use the dwelling place of Peter Delahoi of Guyhirn and the dwelling house of Isaac Culy on the South Brink, Wisbech St. Peter's, as places of worship for Independents (Ely Diocesan Records, B4/4/27, B4/4/35}. Meeting houses for Culimites were observed at the event of the Wisbech Visitation on January 20th 1783. One was at Wisbech, the other at Guyhirn and John Culy was the head of the sect. In the early years of the 19th century Wisbech had a sizeable strength of Sectarists "each provided with a meeting house. They consist of Quakers, Baptists, Anabaptists, Methodists and Culeymites" (An Historical Sketch Of Wisbech, 1809). In about 1827 the Culimites changed their title to Wisbech Calvinists and moved from their old meeting house to the Wool Hall, Exchange Square, Wisbech.

That, then, is the story of the two bishops that introduced Guyhirn, a watery and occasionally flooded place, to the halls of fame.

The River Ouse breaches a bank at Lakenheath in 1912.
(From the Cambridgeshire Collection with permission of Cambridgeshire Libraries)

Flooded farmstead in the Fens.
(From the Cambridgeshire Collection with permission of Cambridgeshire Libraries)

Harvesting from boats near Ramsey, August 1912.
(From the Cambridgeshire Collection with permission of Cambridgeshire Libraries)

The floods on the railway at Littleport, January 1928.
(From the Cambridgeshire Collection with permission of Cambridgeshire Libraries)

WATER THREATENS

Year after year inhabitants of marsh and fen beheld the approach of winter with resignation. In the marsh region flooding by the sea disturbed the outfalls and had the effect of holding back the passage of fresh water from interior fen and the upland. Lutton, Holbeach and Whaplode suffered a severe inundation in 1611 when the incoming tide at a higher level than usual poured over the embankments and drowned the saltmarsh to depths of up to six feet. Reclaimed fertile land was threatened with total submersion. The marsh was treacherous terrain and numerous creeks tended to change course very suddenly as did the circuitous river from the Wash to Wisbech. Parish boundaries and land were very uncertain to determine "for there will be some times a hundred acres of marsh ground, then within a space of three hours the best of it was flooded by the sea . . ."

Reclaiming land from the sea is regarded by some as grossly interfering with nature's intentions; time and again it is proved that man cannot dictate to nature without misfortune in some shape or form. Nature patiently awaits the opportunity to strike back with a vengeance. It happened long ago and happens in our own age. Many times Wisbech was re-visited by huge surges of tidal water urged by severe easterly winds anciently known as the Aegar, forcing the water over the embankment and onto the streets. What happened in recent years reflected the trauma of centuries ago with calamitous loss of life.

In 1236 a terrible flood engulfed Wisbech and almost destroyed the town with its Norman castle. Holinshed described in graphic terms the disaster which occurred "on the morrow after the Feast of Saint Martin and certain days after. The sea burst out with such tides and tempests of wind that the marsh countries near to the sea were drowned and overflown, besides great herds of cattle and flocks of sheep that perished. For two days the sea rose continually, inflowing for the space of two days and a night without ebbing by reason of the mighty violence of contrary winds". On that memorable occasion the sea utterly ruined nearby villages, believed to be Leverington, Newton, the Tydds and Elm, inhabitants drowning in their hundreds. It was recorded that at one village almost a hundred inhabitants perished in a single day. The event was also mentioned by Matthew Paris who recorded: "The sea was raised much higher than usual and the storm continued for eight days, so that men, small ships and cattle, great multitudes perished". The

15

entire Marshland area was re-visited by the sea on many occasions. In 1613 when barely any dry land was visible, the Vicar of Wisbech recorded that many lives had been lost, sea banks broken and the loss of corn crops and cattle was incalculable. Late at night, he wrote, on the Feast of All Saints through the violence of a north-east wind meeting with the tide the sea overflowed the entire area of Marshland with the town of Wisbech, both on the north and the south. Almost the entire Hundred perished to the great danger of life and the loss of some, as well as the loss of corn, cattle and houses which could not be estimated.

The following year on March 23rd it was the turn of freshwater. This came upon Marshland between Wisbech and West Lynn in great abundance, prompted by the extraordinary falls of snow in January and February. The south side of Wisbech succumbed to water incursion but almost all the land within the South Eau bank in South Lincolnshire between Spalding and Tydd St. Giles was rendered useless to farmers for the rest of the year. At the same time Marshland from the bank known as The Edge and the Smeeth to the Podyke was completely submerged following diverse breaches between Salters Lode and Downham Bridge. The lower ground in the old Isle of Ely resembled a vast lake.

Referring to the inundation of 1571, Holinshed recorded that water, several feet deep, quickly spread over vast distances. "The sea broke in between Wisbech and Walsoken and at the Cross Keys, drowning Tilney and Old (West) Lynn". Also badly affected at the time were Wisbech St. Mary, the Tydd villages, Walpole, Walton, Walsoken, Emneth, Jarmans and Stow Bridge, all within ten miles of each other. Neither did Wisbech, Guyhirn, Murrow, Parson Drove and Hobbs Lot escape. It was also mentioned that a church in the flooded area was "drowned" except for the steeple but which village is unrecorded.

West Walton seemed to be a prime target for the water, and the exquisite 13th century church filled with it on several occasions. That its foundations suffered considerably is not in doubt, an expensive underpinning of the walls necessary in modern times to prevent the aisles from collapsing. The floods of old left inhabitants with indelible memories and an ancient tablet in the church perpetrates the trauma experienced by scores of local families.

Surely our sins were tinctured in grain;
May we not say the labour was in vain.
So many washings – still the blots remain.

Everything possible was done to deter floods but the "washings" continued and left their mark uniquely in salt stains on the pillars of local churches. God knows how many people died through the ravages of sea and fresh water. The Fen people, possessors of stoical qualities born of challenge, set about repairing the breaches with rare determination.

In more lenient times the Fens had large acreages of meadowland. In winter the lower shores of the islands were familiarly submerged and the causeways in the marsh temporarily disappeared beneath rising water. In spring this began to recede and where it had covered the shore lush grass grew, offering cattle and sheep sheltered in island harbours rich pasturage. Lowly situated parishes on almost imperceptible gravel ridges as at Fosdyke, Lincolnshire, and the Wiggenhall villages in West Norfolk, all with a tidal river in their backyards so to speak were always at serious risk. Inhabitants accepted the floods as a way of life.

Slightly elevated areas, too low to be defined as islands but which just managed to keep dry when the water rose were known as cotes, places of refuge for cattle and sheep. March, Chatteris, Whittlesey, Coates, Littleport, Stonea and Manea were practically surrounded with pools of water. Through taxation inhabitants were obliged to maintain causeways, repairs carried out in the dry season. Five centuries ago a surveyor of the highways was included in the number of officers responsible for the town of March, his particular task to keep causeways in reasonable repair. The town helped to maintain Aldreth Causeway, near Haddenham, and it suffered the additional burden of being solely responsible for the bridge over the Old West River, a heavy and unfair financial imposition upon the inhabitants. Fen people took full advantage of fisheries which abounded in the interior fens. During the summer numerous small and large pools formed and the task of catching eels became that much easier.

Regular flooding had its advantage and saturated areas useless for husbandry were highly efficient in yielding unbelievable numbers of wild fowl as well as eels and several species of fish, which formed the Fens main economy. It is quite understandable that Fen people spoke with one voice for the retention of their so-called rights to use the wetland profitably and which was bountifully provided with these creatures.

People living in the marsh areas adjoining the coastline experienced the most appalling disasters from sea incursion. On occasions swirling torrents of fresh water combined with that of the sea, and the rivers, unable to discharge into the outfalls, spilled over and water spread rapidly across the marsh. Before the general drainage scheme in the 17th century took effect several unbanked primeval rivers had a tendency to change course, a natural phenomenon in marsh regions. The Fen people relied for their wellbeing on the ancient system of embanked rivers and coastal areas. Several of these old banks can still be traced around Long Sutton, Newton, West Walton and Terrington St. Clement overlooking vast areas of reclaimed land even more devoid of trees than the Fens several miles inland.

Old seabanks dating from Roman times were called "vallum" (wall), and this is reflected in the Anglo-Saxon place names Wal-soken, Wal-ton and Wal-pole. One of the odd yet enriching features of the area, once so frequently washed by water, are the medieval churches built extraordinarily well to impress beholders. These represent the great building styles from the Norman to Perpendicular periods. Somehow they survived the onslaught of storm and water combined and subjected to floods with depths up to six feet. The foundations were usually reinforced with timber rafts, and considering that churches were standing in water for weeks and months at a time, it is indeed a miracle that they stand at all.

Accounts tell of hamlets in the marsh being destroyed by floods. One, apparently called Dolpoon, believed to have been situated in the area of Sutton Bridge, was wiped off the map and presumably most of its inhabitants drowned.

When Dolpoon stood,
Long Sutton was a wood.

This suggests that the disaster helped Long Sutton to prosper. A hamlet known as Saltmarsh, near Newton, was similarly devastated. It had a chapel which was destroyed by the sea. Possibly the hamlet was abandoned and its survivors transferred to Newton. Strange tales relate to Saltmarsh and its chapel, testifying to "bodies anciently buried there in which chapel wondrous *nonnullorum miraculum genera* and shining lights had appeared of old and still appear at night". Another chapel which was left to decay was situated near Parson Drove. It existed in 1107 and an old map of Wisbech Hundred (c. 1540) shows a religious building known as Endewicke. All these buildings and more were ruined or completely destroyed by sea incursion. These forays of nature were so violent, according to witnesses a fishing boat and its crew at work in the 16th century were forced inland

River Ouse at Over 1947; water pours through the breach flooding thousands of acres.

by fierce gales and towering waves and came to rest on the roof of a house. Still aboard, the sailors hearing terrified cries of a pregnant woman from a room beneath them, managed to save her from a watery grave but were, unfortunately, unable to rescue her husband.

Determination existed among Fen people to persevere in the face of disaster and, in the most appalling circumstances, they repaired breached embankments and rebuilt their farms and stock. Then they set out to achieve the unthinkable and began to force the sea from its territory and erect earth barriers to hold it at bay. Despite setbacks this continued in the face of storms and ruinous tidal surge. Nowadays, the flatness of reclaimed grounds where fine crops mature, belies its former state when men and sea were locked in the bitter struggle for possession. Only the soil gives a clue: it is a sandy colour bequeathed by numerous inflows. Look to the horizon and see the church towers which witnessed disaster upon disaster, their lower basements immersed in water for weeks, even months at a time.

It is generally accepted that the Romans erected the earliest sea banks, but most of these barriers were improved and eventually replaced in medieval times. Piled in heaps on the seaward side are large amounts of debris. It is a different world out there, a world of strange sounds and aromas and, when calm prevails there descends a dignified quiet; a heaving of debris beneath one's feet, rippling water slowly raising and lowering the refuse from the sea. It is the unchanged world of embattled Fenmen of long ago.

Saltmarsh was covered with successive layers of silt and gradually became enclosed with high earth bulwarks, some becoming redundant as marsh reclamation continued. After about ten years saltmarsh became fresh marsh and was liberally covered with course grass; it was then added to parish lands. By that time the old sea bank was in a state of decay and the Fenmen built another nearer the shore. Thus in progressive stages the Fenmen proved their high standards of efficiency in land reclamation. Not without hazards, all along the coast embankments were thrown up, some being breached by the sea and being speedily repaired.

Continued reclamation was a contributory cause of severe silting in natural rivers, some changing course and flowing overnight into settled communities. Reclamation was noticeably slower on the north shores of the Wash, whereas it was more rapid on southern shores between Holbeach and West Lynn due to clay deposits accumulating from northern areas.

In the early 17th century Surfleet managed to acquire only 250 acres of saltmarsh, and Leake added a mere thirty acres to parish land. Moulton and Gedney, south of the Wash shoreline were more successful, acquiring no less than 2,554 acres and 2,000 acres respectively.

Requiring a long time to dry out, saltmarsh produced crabgrass, cotton lavender and samphire and eventually the whole area was covered with coarse grass. Low marsh was worth about a penny per acre and high marsh valued at 2d. per acre. The lower price reflected the high risk of flooding. Reclaimed saltmarsh was indistinguishable from other land and simply defined as high and low; they shared the same level. The quality of the grass made the difference and acres were divided by ditches and embankments. Succeeding generations were familiar with increasing changes in the soil and as more land was added to older acres, boundaries continually expanded. This was not always attributed to men's design. In the first quarter of the 17th century farmers took advantage of changing creeks and added more acres to existing saltmarsh. In south Lincolnshire prevailing winds forced new channels through the marsh, a not uncommon occurrence. The River Ouse which had its original outfall near Wisbech was beset with problems by excessive silting and the tributary affected to such an extent that ships entering and leaving the port were imperilled.

Changes in the area's waterways were noticed in the 1570's, creeks becoming so choked with silt as to be unnavigable. Fishermen's wives standing on embankments were in the habit of calling their husbands at sea home to dinner, but within a few years the vessels were unable to approach within a mile of the bank. The provision of fish was a local speciality and very plentiful in saltwater creeks. They were also taken in abundance from the Fens' inland meres and rivers. The economy was quite exceptional and the Fen folk bred large herds of oxen, fine horses and even victualised the royal navy. In 1513-14 two-hundred-and-fifty-three fat winter fed oxen were purchased by the navy victualler from Saltfleet. He also went shopping at Wisbech and purchased 322 oxen and a further 164 animals at Stamford and Peterborough reared on water meadows at these towns.

The men of Holbeach, Long Sutton, Walpole and Terrington tended with great care new and old grazing pasture situated to the rear of the sea banks. Marsh grass was tolerably suitable for cattle, but more especially for horses. Large flocks of sheep turned onto the marsh fared well and that alone introduced additional wealth to the Fens, some farmers helping to finance building and embellishment of exceptionally fine churches for which the Fens and the Marshland in particular are famous. Hundreds of years ago wool from the Fens was considered good and it was cheaper than anywhere else. The Cotswolds produced the best, Suffolk and Norfolk wool rated very good, both counties enjoying great wealth as is evident in the fine churches and timbered buildings to be seen at many towns. Including the Lynn Marshland, East Anglia's beneficial enterprise from the sale of wool is a tribute to the commercial influence of the Hanseatic League, a kind of medieval Common Market but without the politics.

Land reclamation in the vicinity of the Wash is a story of stoical endeavour. Inhabitants of villages and hamlets in the coastal region were subjected to a life of hazardous toil, a fight for survival often against the odds. Physically and financially the demands set against them broke a good many honest, hardworking souls. A survey carried out at Long Sutton in 1609 revealed that "village lands" within or adjacent to the parish were given no fewer than eleven categories. One acre was known as "free increase land"; another "free burgage land" given to tenants. "Dearbought land" was appropriately named as it had long been subjected to floods and workers experienced a trying and costly time wresting it from the sea. When difficulties were insuperably against all sense of reclamation the land was abandoned and used for wildfowling and fishing.

The tenants were obliged to plough "Workland", then sow and reap the crops for the owner usually the lord of the manor. "Conquest land", was so-called because it had finally yielded to workers' efforts, "they having won it by labour and industry from the water which did overflow it". Most tenants had to stack corn and hay, the ground used for this purpose known as "Golving land".

Marshland residences were constantly in danger of being damaged and destroyed by the sea. There were no secure places for families to resort to, except in certain cases the occupation of cold church towers. Those that lived on the Fen islands seldom experienced the trauma of being forced from their homes by torrents of water, although off-island residences could be flooded for weeks in exceptional wintry conditions when more than the usual amounts of fresh water poured into the Fen basin from the uplands. Off-shore islets known as cotes or harbours rose only slightly above the marsh level and offered uncertain refuge for beast. It was known for some cotes to be drowned by large volumes of water with disastrous consequences to owners and stock. Weather dictated the differences between poverty and wellbeing for the Fenmen, and weather certainly imbued inhabitants with a hardness born of uncertainty and despair. It encouraged fortitude and well did the Fen people have need of it. True sons of the Fens are helped by remarkable constitutions and that, in the face of adversity, sometimes earned them the reputation of displaying cantankerous attitudes to strangers.

The islands and outlying marsh served inhabitants tolerably well albeit between inevitable bad patches. Excellent inland communication existed between parishes via rivers and meres and when causeways became impassable in winter the waterways came into their own. Fen meres provided islanders with practically everything needful for their tables, but even those expanses of water, seldom more than four feet deep, could turn inexplicably nasty and vibrate so violently as to overturn boats with loss of life. This peculiar phenomenon regularly occurred at Ramsey Mere and **doubtlessly at other meres, as well. The Fen people were unique and** descended from the Girvii – the water people – observed in Anglo Saxon times. Upland people were inclined to view Fenmen with disdain but the latter's adaptability to harsh conditions which would squeeze the life from ordinary farmers, worked well for island and marsh communities.

Hard going

A lonely Fen road dwarfed by the massive bank of the New Bedford River.

MAKING A LIVING

Fishing and wildfowling was a Fenman's birthright and his way of making a living practised from early Anglo-Saxon times. These were prime occupations especially around the fringe areas where the fen meets the upland. Wildfowl, eels and various species of fish as well as sedge and rushes were conveniently transported along the river system and produce from the interior taken on boats to key places where traders from far distances brought articulated transport to the edge of the Fens. The vehicles hauled by as many as ten or twelve horses were loaded with minimum of delay and taken to cities as much as eighty miles away.

Summer was the ideal time for this business. Fish and eels trapped in meres and in stagnant pools were unable to escape until the rains enlarged the meres and formed new water channels. Sedge, harvested in the frosty season, was stacked and dried in winter then released to buyers in the spring and summer when the material was needed to repair and renew roofs and thatch new homes and barns. Husbandry was practised extensively on the islands and was little different to that on the upland. Crops of corn, peas and beans and herds of cattle and flocks of sheep demanded unstinting labour of their owners. The humble eel, a great asset to the Fen islanders was an important part of the local economy and for centuries used as a means of rent for abbots and bishops, holders of vast estates of marsh, dairy farms woodland and commons. Many fen inhabitants were employed by them. In the 17th and 18th centuries, the main drainage scheme well under way, creatures of the marsh were still in great demand. The fishermen and wildfowlers observed their traditional living diminish and began to suffer as meres dried out and the wildfowl moved to unaffected areas in the country.

Water was the Fenmen's livelihood. In wintertime it poured into the natural basin from surrounding upland, merging small lakes into one, swelling the meres and enabling the Fenmen to pursue his rightful work at the fisheries. Other tasks demanded their attention, too. In 1570 the average Fen farmer possessed eight dairy cattle, a couple of horses, three geese and a pig. His neighbour might well have kept poultry, a breeding mare, four dairy cattle and three swine. When upland farmers put away their ploughs and confined stock to winter quarters, snow covering the fields, men of the Fens welcomed massive amounts of water to places where it naturally accumulated then took advantage of it Come spring and summer, work followed a similar pattern to that experienced in the winter. A writer

22

observed the following in 1690: "As for wildfowl, about midsummer at moulting time, several persons go in small boats among the reeds and knock the birds down with long poles, being then quite unable to swim or fly. As for fish, there are great quantities, especially pike".

In places surrounding the islands, water was nine feet to ten feet deep and fine specimens of fish, not to mention eels, were taken. Geese thrived on the islands where there was plentiful grass but the flavour of wildfowl was said to be both rank and muddy. When fed regularly with corn the flavour changed and the birds equalled any other. Geese feathers were highly valued and the poor creatures were regularly plucked, sometimes six times a year and three for their quills. Geese are hardy creatures and some islanders owned as many as a thousand. Some were kept in cages in the rooms of cottages and it has been said that the owners thought more of them than they did their wives!

The Fenmen had a particular way of preparing fuel. They gathered the dung of oxen and cows, tempered it with water then spread it in layers five inches thick over the ground. These were in oblong pieces a foot long called dithes and stacked up to dry. Dung prepared in this way was also used for making walls. Hogs' dung was similarly treated; the process included stirring it well and it was used to wash clothes which were bleached in summer. The garments appeared white and perfectly clean. As befits the marshy environment, Fen people were constantly troubled with insects such as gnats and midges, the former, known as the "stinging gnat", said to be particularly troublesome. People at Crowland invented a fine mesh, Crowland Sack, draped over beds at night to keep the pests at bay. There were times when the local people cursed the marsh which, apart from providing a living of sorts, devised ways of testing the strongest will. They recognised, however, that the annual "drowning" in a roundabout fashion brought them a fair to good living.

Enclosure of marsh and land took place during the 13th century. One of the earliest records testifies to 280 acres of fen at Somersham and 1,880 acres at Elm being enclosed between 1198 and 1215. Land at Doddington "enclosed with ditches" was let by the Bishop of Ely in 1230, and tracts of land elsewhere were divided with ditches, so obviously efforts were being made long before serious drainage to control egress of water into and through the Fens. At Thorney the monks devised a ring system of dykes to surround the monastery estate and that, in effect, gave them more land to work with. Use of ditches proved helpful but it was mainly through gravitation and lack of rain that enclosed areas could be systematically used by owners and tenants.

In 1294 John Wake of Deeping received objections from tenants that the Prior of Spalding had seen fit to enclose large tracts of marsh amounting to about 80 acres, then encompassed it with a ditch which proved to be a great hindrance to the community, preventing men from entering the commons. In doing so the prior had infringed common law. Leasing out pieces of fen for rent in the 14th century was common practice and Elm excelled, Crowland too, the manorial lands at the latter place greatly affected.

It has wrongly been said that in pre-drainage times the Fenland aspect presented a dreary waste. Nothing is further from the truth. Certainly there were vast areas of oozing mud, stagnant water and obnoxious odours, but the geological nature of the Fens presented various opportunities for inhabitants who knew how to exploit the marsh to very good advantage. Some areas were well flooded and this ascertained that the meres and large pools survived the summer months thereby assuring townships that ready supplies of fish and eels were available whenever required. It was in winter that water spilled from the rivers and meres. Strangers travelling in the Fens wrongly assumed this was the accepted "dreary" picture seen in the Fens in all seasons.

Areas of marsh afforded excellent opportunities for fishing and wildfowling. An abundance of reeds was there for the taking and even the sea shore proved productive, the Fenmen experiencing excellent business from salt pans. The fen interior as opposed to salt marsh was slightly above sea level and utilised in the production of hay, the annual crop benefitting from occasional floods. In summer numerous herds of cattle fattened on water meadows and workers cut turf for keeping the home fires burning. Islands escaped floods and elevated commons were scenes of intensive arable farming, usually corn and peas, some crops thriving particularly well on the lower shores where water had lain over the winter months.

The Fens were particularly noted for fisheries and the region acquired a famous status as regards this industry. That was one of the reasons that so many monasteries were established in the pre-Conquest period and why abbots extended their estates into the marsh. Fish and wildfowl had an eminent place in monastery refectories and were a very useful means in payment of rent. The most important fisheries were at Wisbech, Doddington, March, Stuntney, Little Downham, Whittlesey, Littleport and Ramsey, all these places with a notable environment of watery surroundings. Stuntney fishery produced an average if 24,000 eels per annum and Littleport 17,000. A fishery at Doddington produced no fewer than 27,000 eels on a yearly basis. Outlier places included in manor estates but not necessarily mentioned in records doubtlessly produced thousands of eels, most going to monasteries including East Dereham in the Norfolk upland.

Mention was made of Witelsmare (Whittlesey Mere) in Edward the Confessors time. There the abbot of Ramsey and the abbot of Peterborough each had one boat and the abbot of Thorney two boats. One of Thorney's boats was let to Peterborough monastery, the abbot of which worked his fisheries with two fishermen and held one virgate of land from the abbot of Thorney. In return, Peterborough's abbot gave pasture to Thorney for the well-being of 120 swine. The agreement included a proviso that if the pasture failed, the abbot of Peterborough feeds sixty pigs with corn and finds sufficient timber for one house and a fence to enclose it. He had also the responsibility of maintaining the house. Eels were of paramount importance to the Fens. A "stick" of eels comprised of twenty-five and Lent was the most favoured time of honouring one's rent with "sticks" of these slippery creatures. Sometimes thieves went into the fisheries at night as happened at Wellenheath near Littleport, one John Beysteus illegally carrying forth fish. He was discovered and threatened with removal from the village.

The peat lands produced large amounts of reed and sedge used for thatching and other building purposes, such as lining the wall cavities and filling in gaps between floors. Medieval workers, villeins for instance, had to cut several bundles of reed in a single operation. At Little Downham, fourteen acres of reed bed was used for rental purposes and earned 4d. per year. Other manors paid 6d., half virgates 3d. and cottars 2d. Cutting the material was carried out at "competent and reasonable times of the year" in order to avoid injuring the fisheries. Complex laws and regulations set out terms for working at the reed beds and occasionally Fenmen abused them.

Harvesting sedge at Littleport was a very prolific undertaking. Seventeen thousand acres were involved, 16,000 acres entirely sedge, all of which formed 90% of the village's economy. Disputes were quite frequent. It was written that John Curtneys and John Gardhant slandered Hugh Beld's sedge

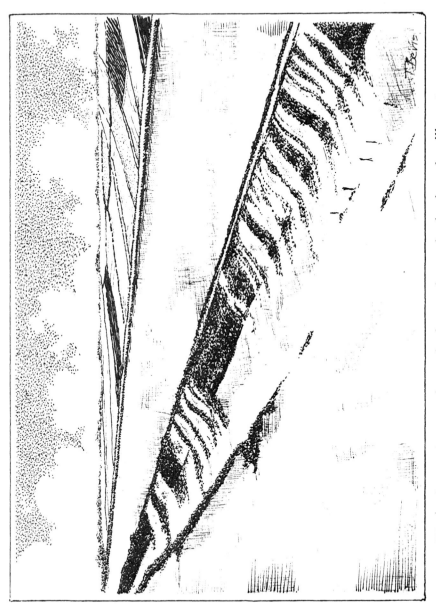

Water forces its way beneath the track on the bank and spills onto farmland and the London–King's Lynn railway line.

A flooded section of the Bedford washland at Earith. The outline of the 17th century sconce built during the Civil War is clearly seen.

and as a consequence Hugh lost the sale of the sedge. Another man, John Fox, "trespassed against John of Elm and purloined nine hundreds of sedge and would not return them". The said Mr. Fox delivered to John Mountfort one thousand sedge of inferior quality than he bought of him and lost eighteen pence. Harvesting of sedge on a commercial basis continued well into the 19th century and the fringe area of Whittlesey Mere was very productive, much of the material sold to people living on the upland.

The lives of the marsh people actively engaged in the silt area near the coast were noticeably different to those living on and around the islands. One occupation was that of managing salt pans occasionally mentioned in the Domesday Book (1086) which alludes to the Wash areas of Norfolk and Lincolnshire. Embankments were raised and salt marsh reclaimed, the sea slowly receding, leaving places such as Holbeach, Long Sutton and Gedney a few miles inland. Several salt pans developed in the marsh but not all of them effectively produced salt. In Holland, Lincolnshire, several villages had salt pans and brisk trade was experienced at towns such as Spalding.

Norfolk Marshland, too, possessed prolific salt pans and these were mentioned in the working of three manors which enjoyed a good enquiry for salt on the upland near Roydon involving a number of villages which were linked to the economy of the salt trade. These villages were responsible for profits among owners and workers employed at the salt pans. At Terrington St. Clement rent from salt pans was paid to abbots and bishops of Ely in "bledes, wayes and gates of salt". Salt pans were occasionally damaged and great care was taken to repair them. The salt trade was closely related to the cutting of turf which was used as fuel to evaporate the brine. Certain areas in the Fens were reserved for supply of turves to associated salt pans; from this will be acknowledged the strong, economic connections which existed with turf digging and extraction of salt.

Fleet with neighbouring villages relied on protection from the sea of substantial banks beyond which lay vast stretches of sand regularly washed by tides. According to a terrier of the village made in about 1315, much activity took place at the pans. Within the sea walk were certain holdings *(hoga et area)* for which rent was paid in salt. A worker known as a bondman paid a toll to the lord of the manor every time he boiled salt outside the village. The lord claimed a toll on all salt sold and received one penny per twenty measures. A measure was called *overgongmiddas* and half a measure was required if the bondman boiled salt within the village. The trade was quite considerable at Fleet, Gedney and Holbeach and bushels of salt from these villages were taken to a "holy place" called *le mothow* which lay outside the sea wall. It was there that the lord gave his approval of each bushel having the correct measure. Incorrect measures were recorded and suppliers were expected to amend errors. Salt making continued in the coastal area all through the Middle Ages and some pans continued in use for some time after that. A declaration made in 1562 stated "much salt is made in England as of sand and water in Hollande in Lincolnshire". It was not until after 1670 that the salt industry in the silt zone went into sharp decline, rock salt being discovered in that year.

Bank burst   T.Bevis

A HAZARDOUS AND DEBILITATING LIFE

Strangers travelling through the Fens between the 13th and 18th centuries were struck by the differences between the upland and the lowland. In the Fens there were obnoxious vapours and most writers and chroniclers recorded that the natives regularly suffered from ague and rheumatic conditions of all kinds. The atmosphere was permanently moist, not an unnatural expectation, the area having an abundance of stagnant pools and meres. The population was known to be cantankerous and argumentive and this was put down to the harsh environment in which they lived. They were hardy amphibians and it was as well that they were as they constantly struggled to maintain some sort of existence against the intentions of their ancient enemies, the rivers and sea.

Yet for all that the region had its finer points. There were abundant grazing lands far richer in content than those on the upland which were frequently subjected to lengthy periods of drought. Seldom did the Fen people have worries about obtaining food, the local meres and waterways superbly endowed with fish and fowl. Sedge and reed were particularly important and used for domestic purposes and large amounts sold to people living on higher ground. Thousands of sheep occupied the salt marsh and grazed on island commons and herds of cattle filled the rich grazings on the lower shores.

Fenmen and Marshmen were not really races apart from their contemporaries on the upland, but ordinary farmers of very special qualities bred into each succeeding generation by a demanding environment. They acquired a hardy constitution and were, for most part, rendered practically immune from serious illness. They acquired ingrained knowledge and possessed a fine sense of anticipation and instinct empowering them to watch and guard against encroachment of river and sea, and they were even able to turn floods to advantage.

Fenmen acted as guides to travellers, cutting corners across the marsh along routes known only to them and which only the foolhardy would attempt alone. Many people unfamiliar with these hazardous routes sank into quicksand and perished or were lost in the fogs and died through exposure in bitterly cold, wet conditions. In some places bells were tolled at dusk to guide travellers to safe ground. Groups en route to places in the Fens, or beyond, assembled at Long Sutton to await the arrival of guides who offered their services for a fee. The majority of professional guides lived at Walpole St. Andrew and Terrington St. Clement and had worked in the marsh and fishing grounds and developed a knowledge of the area.

Marketing was an important asset of marsh communities' internal business, but small when compared with the larger, opulent towns like Wisbech, Long Sutton, Holbeach and Spalding. A fair-sized marsh town in the mid-16th century had between 150-180 families. Each township had a market, even the smaller communities with about 80 families, and commercial transactions were sufficiently sustained as to promote interest beyond the respective parish boundaries.

The original layout of fields in the Fens did not differ fundamentally from those in upland areas. Villages established on the silt belt found enough dry land for developing crops. It was known as "townlands" and arable fields were progressively set out by increasing populations and followed the contours of the shore line. The land extended into the river-flooded plain towards the fen interior where it merged with peat soil. Meadows and pasture were plentiful and in good time the parish boundaries encompassed a rectangular shaped or an elongated area of land. Unlike the upland, arable farming was limited but in the Fens there was an abundance of grazing land. Between the 11th and 16th centuries the population made increasing demands on the resources of fen and marsh. This progress was balanced by the incursory action of the sea and fresh water floods. Men's efforts to drain areas was constant and there was always the opportunity to expand.

The defined shape of most parishes in the Marshland between Terrington and Boston were similar and had a comparatively narrow sea frontage. The hinterland, however, was of great depth as will be observed with Gedney and Gedney Hill several miles inland. Soil differed in quality and that farthest inland where the silt merged with peat and was subjected to flooding from waters from the Midlands was noticeably virile. On the seaward side of embankments the saltmarsh was covered with water at every tide. Sea deposits accumulated against the barriers and in time became higher and free of inundation. It was then ready to be enclosed. After about ten years the salt marsh became fresh marsh and tender grass grew. It was amalgamated with village lands and separated from the old sea bank, a new bank being thrown up nearer the sea. This system of reclamation was employed along the entire Wash shoreline and eventually the sea lost part of its old domain.

In the reign of James the First it was not unusual for inhabitants to discover cockleshells two or three feet deep on the landward side of the sea bank. Occasionally the sea won back its former ground and at Wainfleet, Friskney and Wrangle an inquiry revealed that these parishes could offer no defence against sea incursion other than a natural rise in the ground formed by salt hills. Most of the older sea banks were destined for destruction and washed away by continual erosion. At one coastal village in Lincolnshire where the old sea bank could still be seen, the land in between it and the new bank was described as manor land "gained from the town by the sea".

Strangers unfamiliar with the great expanse beheld fen and marsh as a single piece all of one level. There were differences and local people were well familiar with the various qualities of grass growing on high and low marsh, broken by ridges, banks, ditches, shelves and falling and rising of ground. These stages marked out the stages of land reclamation. The highest marsh was that next to the sea and it quickly drained after spring tides. It was built up with deposits of silt. The low marsh shrank because of frequent inundation. The marsh was intersected with numerous creeks and inlets, some so deep and wide it was possible for small ships to pass into and out of them. The farther the sea receded the more prone the creeks were to silting and before 1570 they had become unnavigable. At Frampton in 1615 it was known by old inhabitants for ships sailing up the creek forty years previously to discharge their cargoes within "two shutts" of the old sea bank. Later they could not get within a mile of it. Henry Mell, an old marshman, could remember the low water mark move in his lifetime from a quarter of a mile of the sea bank to a mile away.

John Orden of Holbeach wrote that a salt water creek at Whaplode had its course so near the sea bank fishermen's wives could stand on it and call their husbands home to dinner. People living at Whaplode who could walk along the old sea bank had then to preamble to their destination a mile farther away. No-one could predict the tide which badly silted up creeks, and salt marsh, formerly abandoned by the sea, changed into its playground again. Rivers within a few miles of the sea were apt to change course in the marsh. Near Wisbech marsh cottages, some distance away from the river, were drowned when overnight its course changed and the river pursued a new path through the marsh and into the buildings. At Walpole and Holbeach spring tides were expected to flood the saltmarsh right up to the seawall at least once a month. Both townships witnessed violent tides in 1611 and the saltmarsh was covered with three feet of water.

When spring tides had drained the marsh, it was necessary for several showers to wash the sand and deplete its salt content. Following this the marsh became suitable for sheep and horses and the grass was of excellent quality. Due to the fact that the marsh could be flooded at any time its value remained relatively low. In 1607 jurors at Gedney explained how "the numbringe of acres is a verie uncertaine thynge for us to doe, for there will be sometymes a hundrethe acres of marsh ground, and within three howers space the best of it will be overflowed with the sea above six foote deep". Shepherds instinctively knew when strong tides were imminent. In accordance with their experience shepherds at Holbeach chose to build cottages at the upper end of the salt marsh where they could best observe the behaviour of the sea. At the close of the 16th century all the high marsh in certain parishes had been enclosed and, in some places, had been sold to individuals. Enclosure of former salt marsh was common during the reign of James the First, and fields bounded by dykes were given new names such as Seafield and Newdykefield.

There was much controversy over drainage in the 17th century. Owners and tenants of marsh and fen vigorously opposed plans to transform the marsh into arable and pasture, the reason being that their so-called rights to take fish and wildfowl would be impaired if not entirely ruined. The sale of reed and sedge minimised in this way would introduce decline for the local economy. As a result poverty would descend upon the inhabitants. The Fenmen published valid reasons as to why they should be left alone to pursue traditional employment and they vehemently objected to propaganda mounted by the drainage capitalists who favoured the scheme.

"The Undertakers", wrote the Anti-Projector in about 1645, "have alwaies vilified the Fens, and have misinformed many Parliament men that all the Fens is a meer quagmire, and that it is a level hurtfully surrounded and of little or no value but those which live in the Fens and are neighbours to it, know the contrary.

"For the first the Fens breed infinite number of serviceable horses, mares and colts which till our land and furnish our neighbours.

"Secondly we breed and feed great store of cattle, and we keep great dayeries, which afford great store of butter and cheese to victual the Navy, and multitudes of heifers and Scots and Irish cattle have been fatted on the Fens, which afford hides and tallow.

"Thirdly, we mow off our Fens fodder, which feeds our cowes in winter, which being housed, we gather such quantities of compost and dung, that it enriches our pastures and corn ground, half-in-half, whereby we have the richest and certainest corn land in England, especially for wheat and barley, whereby by Sea we do, and can (if our navigable rivers be not made unserviceable by the undertakers pernitious new ditches) abundantly furnish London and the northern parts in their necessities. All of which fore-recited commodities make our Fens far more profitable to the owners, lying as they are for grass, then if they were sown with corn, rape or coleseed.

"Fourthly, we keep great flocks of sheep upon the Fens.

"Fifthly, our Fens are a great relief, not onely to our neighbours the uplanders, but to remote Counties which otherwise some years thousands of cattle would want food.

"Sixthly, we have great store of Osier, Reed and Sedge, which are such necessaries as the Counties (but) want them for many uses, and sets many poor on work.

"Lastly, we have many thousand Cottagers which live on our Fens, which otherwise must go a begging. So that if the undertakers take from us a third part of our Fens, they destroy not onely our pastures and corn ground, but also our poor, and utterly disable us to relieve them.

"What is Coleseed and Rape, they are but Dutch commodities, and but trash and trumpery, and pills land, in respect of the fore-recited commodities, which are rich Oare of the Commonwealth".

Straight-speaking propaganda indeed, but it was questioned by Christopher Merret, surveyor of the port of Boston, who, carefully avoiding bias of any kind, recorded in 1696 "several observables in Lincolnshire not noticed by Camden or any other author". The portion of the fenland in which fish and fowl abounded lay in the East Fen between Wainfleet and Sibsey. "For the rest," he wrote, "the fens abound no less with quadrupeds, as beasts, sheep especially and horses".

The drainage undertakers set up a showpiece in Deeping Fen, between Spalding and Crowland, and grew on the carefully drained and prepared land "very great crops of oats and also large quantities of Rapsum Sylv. (called

Coleseed) whereof they make oil". A century later little change had occurred in the economy and in 1698 the breeding of cattle and grazing grounds continued to play a major role in the Fens contribution to the nation's wellbeing.

Livestock was of prime importance to the Fenmen. His status and his place in the economical scale was recognised in the number of cattle he kept. A farmer in Leicestershire had an average herd of six between 1500 and 1530 but in the Fens his counterpart kept ten. In the first thirty years of the 16th century twenty out of a hundred Leicestershire farmers had no cattle whereas in the Fens hardly four in a hundred were without herds. Fen farmers kept an average of ten cattle and a really large herd in the first half of the 1500's numbered forty. The farmer of average fortune possessed anything between five and seventeen animals and most of these were dairy cows.

The dairying aspect of farming in the ancient Fens was of great importance and considerably enhanced the standing of a farmer in the locality. The better-off farmer with butter and milk vessels, a cheese press and cheese vats enjoyed enviable status in the community. When a farmer died, such as John Hood of Sutterton, Lincolnshire in 1537, his fortune was four times the average. This was measured in his effects amounting to ten stones of cheese and two stones of butter waiting to be sold. Even the poorer farmer classed as a peasant did reasonable well. Henry Wythington of Tydd St. Mary in 1537 had property valued at £4 10s. 4d. (after deduction for debts) and his store contained ten stones of cheese.

Nine out of ten Fen farmers kept horses in the 1530's. In the upland regions oxen continued to be employed on farms and this was the tendency in the Fens as land was not sufficient for six horses of the average farmer. Horses bred in the Fens were sold at upland markets. One farmer, John Hynde, had 22 (eight horses, five foals, six mares and three fillies), equal to his cattle. Undoubtedly this man was a breeder.

The Fenland economy relied a great deal on sheep, but Fen wool was never rated as fine as other English wools. Its value was a little more than Norfolk wool which was the cheapest of all. However the Fen farmer did well from the sale of sheepskins, for was not a "Fenman's dowry three score geese and a pelt?" A quarter of the farmers had no sheep at all but those with more than sixty sheep were twice as well off as the average. Often the well-to-do declined to keep sheep. The inventories of the 1530's tell us that

Thomas Thornton of Tydd St. Mary owned 120 sheep, less than half the size of the biggest flocks in Leicestershire. Provincial inventories are not very helpful as regards stockholdings since the wills of wealthy people were proved in London and not locally. A small number of sheep owners in Leicestershire had fewer than twenty sheep and half the flocks kept in the Fens were equal. There were multitudes and even the poorest peasant kept a few sheep, a horse and one or two cows and sustained them on the commons.

Between 1530 and 1600 most Fen farmers owned on average ten cattle, four pigs, six horses and twenty sheep. One man, Roger May, who died in 1537 possessed seven cattle, three swine, six mares and twenty sheep and his property valued at £11 18s. 9d. Another farmer who died in about 1566 owned five kyne and two calves, two mares, three foals, a pig, fourteen ewes and six lambs and a cock and ten hens. Certain inventories of the 1560's and 1590's refer to "pullen", which were ducks, hens and geese. In the 1530's only two in five people kept poultry. A typical farmer, John Baker the elder, had six kine, four calves, one quy and four burlings. All fifteen cattle were dairy animals. His holding also comprised five pigs and twenty-three sheep and a couple of horses. After £5 debts had been deducted the holding was valued at £45.

Changes in the Fenland became more pronounced during the 16th century, mainly due to the pace. The main problem in South Lincolnshire and the Norfolk Marshland was similar to that experienced in the Midlands: a shortage of adequate pasture and commons. The Crown took a sudden interest in the Fens at the beginning of the 17th century, particularly in the gains of the saltmarsh which was very considerable all along the coast. As a result villages in south Lincolnshire lost most of their saltmarsh commons and it was observed that some parts of the Fenland had entered into a state of deterioration. This was because drains were being neglected and enclosures began to squeeze at the edges of the remaining saltmarsh.

The population of the Fens and saltmarsh areas in the 16th century and early 17th century was quite large and many poor people depended entirely on their common rights for a livelihood. This was gradually being erased and the profits awaiting the large grazier with ever increasing stock of animals proved very attractive. The grant of the saltmarsh of four parishes in Elloe wapentake to the Earl of Argyle in 1615 outlined the Crown's concern for the "recovery, including and defending of the marsh, as well for the common good and profit of our commonwealth". A great deal of effort by the undertakers to persuade Fen people to support the drainage scheme had some affect on the large farmers and several of their workers joined the undertakers in their attempts to drain large tracts of fen. However, the Fenmen, most of whom were small farmers, were generally against the scheme. Wildfowlers and fishermen depended a great deal on the product of natural, unspoilt fen for their livelihood. Thomas Fuller sized up the problem pretty well: "Grant them drained, and so continuing; as now the great fishes therein prey on the less, so then wealthy men would devour the poorer sort of people. Injurous partage would follow upon the enclosures, and rich men, to make room for themselves, would jostle the poor people out of their commons".

There was much dispute and certain constructive proposals were put forward to settle the disturbances in South Lincolnshire. Fen abuses were enumerated but were not mentioned in the Exchequer depositions. The wealthy farmers with sizeable pastures on which to sustain their sheep in winter, overcrowded the commons in summer. Some had as many as a thousand sheep and argued that if they were obliged to charge their commons with but two hundred sheep and the children and servants of commoners had no common rights, the problem affecting the grazing shortage would be solved overnight.

Fenmen with large flocks of geese, for instance as many as a thousand, were the cause of arguments as much of the fen was comparatively dry and the geese supposedly soiled the ground and cattle and horses were deprived of the sweetest grass. It was suggested that each commoner might keep at the most sixty geese.

A varied number of crops were grown in the Fens between 1530 and 1600. Crops were grown sparsely and several farmers had no arable at all, and others possessed small plots devoted to spring corn, and nothing else. Store chambers accommodated reserves of beans, wheat and barley and farmers purchased considerable supplies of fodder and cereals for domestic use.Where arable was divided between spring and winter corn, some farmers turned their attention to the growing of barley, wheat, beans and peas grown on the bulk of the land. Barley was the most important crop and occupied an average of fifty-four per cent of the sown area. Inventories reveal that between thirty-five and forty per cent of Fen farmers had barley in store, regardless of whether or not they had crops in the field. Some corn was sold to the ale houses of London in 1573 and 1574, therefore it was likely that the avid beer drinkers of that city owed thanks to the barley growers of the Fens.

Beans and peas ranked second in importance and occupied about 28 per cent of the sown area. Eventually peas gave way to beans and became the most important of the two crops. The Fen farmer devoted three barley lands to every one of beans and peas, hay being then the principal mainstay of the Fen grazier in winter. It was ideally suited to the fen and grew abundantly. The Fen inhabitants' winter diet was supplemented by beans and peas held in store. Wheat was third in importance to barley and beans and was ideally suited to silt lands. It was not an essential crop for farmers and bread made from wheat was considered a luxury. According to the "Anti-Projector" wheat grown on the Fen land was exported to London and to the north of England. About six out of ten Fen farmers with arable land grew some wheat amounting to about nine per cent of the sown area. The poorer peasants were better suited with barley or rye bread.

An exceptional crop, oats are mentioned only once in inventories and rye was slightly more important. A quarter of the farmers saw fit to grow little more than two per cent of oats on the sown area. The Fens' great speciality, hemp, occupied about 14 per cent of the sown area in the 1560's. One in three inventories mention the crop but not every farmer grew it. It formed a subsidiary occupation to agriculture on the majority of farms, flax, hemp, linseed and, of course, a linen wheel were regularly listed in the wills relating to farmers' personal property.

From this it will be acknowledged that the Fen people lived reasonably well, better in fact than many farmers on the surrounding uplands. The price however was considerable when considering the constant battle against the elements and the forays of the sea and wide-spread inundation and effects of fresh water. Floods overturned progress but the Fen people were a match for nature's mischievous antics and even took advantage of distressing situations. Even in modern times water incursion introduced untimely reminders to the Fens' inhabitants of those calamitous visitations which occurred in the region long ago, and certainly no less devastating than the great floods of 1947 still in living memory.

THE FLOODS OF 1947

The unruly elements that struck Britain in 1947 brought in their wake an unwelcomed aspect of the Fens of four and five centuries ago. Pure horror of drowned land, of farm dwellings and buildings through which water flowed and indeed, some actually collapsed, the victims saved from roofs and others fleeing for their lives to higher ground. It was referred to as the Black Winter, a title which the author thinks is a gross understatement. Thousands of acres were utterly inundated and damages and loss of a colossal nature amounted to £20,000,000, amazing even when compared with increases relating to similar problems affecting the country in 2000 and 2001. The Fen disaster of 1947 mirrors the terrible trauma experienced by the Fen people hundreds of years ago.

Of the national acreage subjected to deluge in 1947 the Fens submitted 71,000 acres to water incursion and it was estimated that many thousands of acres devoted to winter corn were destroyed and about 21,000 tons of potatoes ruined. The floods were prompted by huge falls of snow shifted by powerful winds in drifts five to six feet high. The gales were the strongest ever known in the Fens and the weather very cold, so bitter that birds froze to their perching places and small animals froze into blocks of ice, some buried six feet or more beneath masses of frozen snow. As far as the Fens were concerned the real danger amounted to huge volumes of water released by the thaw and, in the month of March, the rivers began taking unbelievable amounts of water which rose to alarming levels against river banks. It was then that the Fen people's worst fears were realised. The huge embankments for which the Fens are renowned were beset with tremendous pressures and, unable to contend with masses of water pouring into the Fen basin from the thaw affecting snow-covered upland as well as the Fens' own snow-clad fields. The rivers discharged water over the banks and through torn-out gaps in unstoppable torrents.

This continued night and day and the news heard in disbelief in several villages, people gathering what possessions they could and fleeing the encroaching mass of water which rapidly engulfed isolated farmsteads. Dykes disappeared from view as the floods raced across virile fields, devouring everything in the way. Homes were assailed and residents, left with no time to prepare, forced to move upstairs with anything which could be carried out of the reach of the water. The ground floor rooms filled with water to a height just below the ceilings and the frightened occupants were forced to climb out of the windows onto the roofs and hold on literally for dear life. A correspondent wrote: "The wind shrieked across the flat countryside, blowing down trees, scattering the roofs of haystacks and tossing the tiles from farm buildings. Men on the banks watched the rising floods. The wind piled against the banks until the water began to flow, slowly at first and then in torrents from one embankment to the next".

In the 1947 disaster, as well as many previous floods in the Fens, men worked without sleep and they simply sat down and slumbered for a short while. Most livestock was moved to high ground, the Fen islands perceived as safe places and reverting to their ancient status as winter harbours. Fenmen have an unerring instinct of pending disaster and many farmers had already moved cattle to higher ground thereby averting serious loss among the herds. The writer remembers standing on the old bridge at Guyhirn watching men with long poles easing odd cattle caught in the floods beneath the bridge. They were floating, legs aimed grotesquely at the forboding sky, and were prone to be snagged on the archways. Once free of the obstacle the powerful current carried the carcases through Wisbech and into the Wash some eighteen miles away. I cycled to Crowland to view the floods, the famous old town virtually becoming an island again as the River Welland stealthily encroached upon the parish. It was an error of judgement when, six hours later, I turned my wheels towards Thorney only to find the road covered with water. Eventually I made my way to March via the Deepings and to Peterborough, many more miles than was intended.

Breaches on the Welland bank near Crowland were filled with surplus army vehicles and thousands of sandbags piled against them until time came when the breaches could be better dealt with. In reality, once a breach occurs the water will run its course and the level beyond the bank will rapidly fill. Despite portable pumps being used absolutely nothing can be done to reverse the situation. Livestock suffered appallingly and hundreds of pigs and thousands of chickens perished. More than six hundred families vacated their houses in a single day. It was then that the wisdom of making roads on the embankments was appreciated and, at least, hundreds of people forced to abandon their homes were able to move along them to safety, viewing as they went thousands of acres of water where the fields had been. That is the one great advantage of the Fens. If a flood does happen, exit routes exist, whereas on the natural flood plains in the north and south of the country where planning departments authorised new buildings, a significant rise in the water level can spell disaster to roads as well as people and property

In the 1947 disaster practically everyone living in the affected areas were engaged in the struggle to save whatever they could and endeavour to plug breached banks where threat of widespread flooding was greatest. The army was enlisted to help and military personnel and prisoners-of-war were brought to the Fens and worked alongside Fire Service personnel armed with portable pumps; the Dutch government mindful of their own personal experiences of floods sent a pontoon crane. The water permeated the land and spread into solid foundations and many buildings collapsed. Walls cracked and roofs and bricks fell into the water until eventually hardly any sign was left of the buildings. Furniture moved into upper chambers was ruined and floated away over the fields. For miles around the aspect resembled the sea and here and there piles of debris gathered, illustrative of the destructive powers of nature. It is true to say that every house on the affected plains was touched by the floods. The view from nearby Ely sprawling on its hill eighty feet above the great level was sobering, almost 15,000 acres of prime agricultural land submerged, reflecting devastation on a hitherto unknown scale.

A huge gap was torn into the bank near Earith and water poured through, covering roads leading to several villages. The scene from the tower of Haddenham church resembled that of the time when local hero, Hereward the Wake, assembled his forces near adjacent Aldreth to confront his adversary William the Conqueror. Here some 6,000 acres remained inundated until mid-summer. To make matters worse a permanent pump unit broke down and in desperation an antique steam pump fired up and brought into service. It was stopped when the boiler threatened to explode and other machinery parts more than a hundred years old failed. The water triumphed and raced into the fen. Workmen laboured to position a makeshift dam and secure it, only to see later that night water topping the bank. A steam pump worked on and ran short of coal and fuel was hastily transferred by vehicles and a horse and cart from a broken engine to the one still remaining. Fenmen battled on without sleep and were reinforced by hundreds of German prisoners-of-war who were sent to the banks and deployed in every way to contain the waters. Yet still the Hundred Foot river continued to rise and sand bags had to be built around the isolated engine to protect it.

A helpful factor was absence of gales. The Fens had everything wrong happening but the wind held back until the 16th; then the gale swept in and scooped water, throwing it over the bank. Trees fell over and impeded efforts to rescue something worthwhile from this terrifying ordeal. Men were unable to stand and reduced to crawling around. Efforts at Over to minimise the situation had to be abandoned after a section about sixty feet wide was torn from the bank. Everything possible that men could do was tried but the forces of nature ruled otherwise. She really displayed her prowess at destruction along the Old West River and water poured into the flatlands on a front of about two miles, filling the fen with a calculated 70,000,000 tonnes of water. So much, in fact, that the struggling pumps could not cope and had to be shut down. The engine at Haddenham was utterly overcome by fierce running torrents, the water making a mockery of its purpose by actually covering the pump house.

This, then, was the story emerging from the Fens in 1946-47, the national newspapers telling a story of unbelievable horror and lauding the stoical attitudes of the Fen people. The medieval aspect had visited the Fens yet again and people really could not understand why it had happened to a region protected in such a way as to make flooding on such a scale, as they thought, a thing of the past. Despair and devastation not only descended upon Crowland and Haddenham and other places it affected the whole of the Fens. As evidenced in previous centuries the Fen spirit, strongest when confronted with lengthening odds, served the region well, the population grappling admirably with drowned fields, broken barns, ruined dwellings, useless machinery and great loss of stock.

The great flood of 1946-47 was certainly not the first major inundation to happen in the Fens but on this occasion it was not expected, whereas centuries ago the Fenmen, to some extent, were prepared for these things and knew what to do. People reasoned with some justification that the modern Fens protected with specially designed drains, a myriad of dykes, massive sluices and numerous pumps of varying capacities, ought never to be subjected to such devastation. Damage caused by the Great Flood was colossal, as much as £13,000,000 required to put things on something resembling an even keel. Crops, particularly potatoes, lay rotting on sodden fields. It was probably the worst flood to happen in the Fens for four hundred years and the destruction of so much of what was recognised as the nation's larder affected the whole country which relied heavily on Fen produce.

Arguments as to why the floods occurred flew in all directions. Drainage experts were blamed and also agricultural committees and catchment boards, none apparently having foreseen the possibility of such a disaster. Farmers argued that people employed to oversee protective measures had never driven a tractor or used a spade and could not be familiar with farmers' requirements if they were to continue tilling the land in the knowledge that they were adequately protected from floods. A flood of such magnitude should not have been possible, they said, and the blame, in part, rested with the academics sitting at office desks. It was argued that the qualifications these officers held were not the answer and they had neglected to speedily put into place a fool-proof anti-flood system to cope with such emergencies occurring on what is, after all, a natural flood plain much of which lies beneath sea level and obviously requires an unquestionably efficient drainage system. In an area as low as the Fens it is vitally necessary to have sufficient catchment areas with enough sluices to hold water in check against tides. An astonishing amount of water from surrounding uplands and the Midlands flows into the Fen basin and this has happened for more than fifteen hundred years. It is a phenomenon that will probably never change but, if anything, given time climatic changes will contribute to increases in the water volume in most parts of the country.

After 1947 it became glaringly obvious that a relief river was necessary to assist the many desired improvements which had to be added to the existing drainage system. Prior to the great flood, many improvements had materialised but nothing like enough. Rivers had been widened and deepened and even insignificant streams along which upland water found its way into the great Fen basin had taken on a greater purpose in the overall design to discharge water from the Fens more speedily into the outfalls. Prime consideration had to be given to the propulsion of water in upland areas and eject it from the Fens as quickly as possible. Planning had failed in ascertaining that the Fens had sufficient machinery, pumps, sluices and catchment drains to move water in exceptionally wet seasons or hold it back as and when required. Nineteen-forty-seven proved that something had to be done to prevent such a thing happening again.

Accordingly, a new relief river was cut on the east side of the Fens at a cost of about £7,000,000. One of the greatest assets in the Fens in the perpetual struggle to diminish risk of serious flooding are washes at Earith, Cowbit, Welney and at Whittlesey where thousands of acres of grazing land are allowed to flood at appropriate times. It is conceivable that even more washland areas will be required with the possibility of greater volumes of water pouring into the Fens. With foresight, a lot of things could have been done before 1947, but, as is usually the case, bureaucracy prevailed and ancient wisdom in these matters relegated to the back burner. Experienced farmers were aware that in exceptional times when the heavens open dramatically and combine forces in black and white, it makes sense to hold water back then release it gradually, the land absorbing most. The planners' idea was to eject the water far too quickly and, as it happened, with dire results. The effect of large falls of snow was not contemplated and nothing was done to combat the effects of a rapid thaw.

I began writing this in the year 2000 and finished in 2001, the years when the country was visited with floods of great severity. These occurred in the west, the north and the south of England, the unbanked rivers spilling over dramatically, flooding towns, villages and isolated dwellings, creating appalling damage to railway lines, roads, personal property and livestock and much more besides. Nowadays planning authorities tend to allow houses to be built on flood plains of old standing. Most rivers, except those in the Fens, have no high banks and the usual level of water has only to rise slightly before spreading unrestricted over a vast area. .

We seem to have entered a phase of unusually wet conditions, brought about it is said by the greenhouse effect, soaking the land to such an extent that water has nowhere to go except lay on the surface. Building on flood plains does not help, concrete foundations limiting the natural soakway and allowing water to spread freely across the plain. Providing embankments is a hugely expensive operation and almost prohibitive on a large scale where flooding occurred recently in other areas of the country. Furthermore those affected regions have no sophisticated drainage system to discharge water into tidal rivers, there being few if any pumps or large areas of washland as seen in the Fens and which is acknowledged a well tried means of storing vast amounts of water. These grass areas have no buildings set upon them and excessive water finds its way into tidal rivers at the appropriate time, thence via controlled sluice gates it is discharged safely into the sea.

I like to think that in the Fens we have learned lessons from the past and applied the yardstick of people's embittered struggle and failure to establish as near as humanly possible a foolproof system of ejecting unwanted water from reclaimed grounds. It has taken more than 400 years to do that and the expense has been colossal. The Fenmen of old, repeatedly engaged in throwing up embankments and digging drains simply to survive would marvel at the water gates, embanked rivers, sophisticated pumping machinery and deliberately flooded acres. They would approve.

FLOODS . . .
WHAT WILL HAPPEN NOW?

Severe flooding in the west country, in the north of England and in the south of the country raises the spectre of repetition on a scale perhaps even more intensified than has ever been experienced in the Fens. The greenhouse effect is probably responsible for recent inundations but there is more to it than that. It is quite possible that two centuries ago the same thing happened in other areas and possibly in the same places. There have always been natural flood plains and in past centuries seldom were these built upon.

Where, then, is the country's most efficiently drained area and can lessons be learned from it? The answer lies in the Fens. Skirting the Wash from Boston to King's Lynn and stretching many miles inland, touching the "island" towns of Ely, March, Whittlesey, Chatteris and Wisbech, the latter built over the centuries on medieval seabanks, by all rights if any part of the country is to become a lake, the Fen country more than qualifies. Two-thirds of the Fens are uncomfortably below sea level and parts imperceptibly above. An "island" in the Fens was anciently a valued place of refuge offering sanctuary to the water people in the Saxon and medieval eras.

Flowing through low levels made up of silt and peat the rivers Witham, Glen, Welland, Nene and the Great Ouse discharge into the Wash with tidal surge. They are harnessed to a very sophisticated drainage system which has taken more than 500 years to evolve. Like a giants spider's web a radial system of numerous man-made dykes and drains directly and indirectly linked to natural rivers collect water from a vast expanse of agricultural land. The rivers also have to cope with water from surrounding upland spilling into the Fen basin from Northamptonshire, Bedfordshire, Lincolnshire and Norfolk.

Divided into three separately administrated levels, North, Middle and South, hundreds of manual and automatic pumps scoop water and pass it into the rivers and main drains where eventually it is emptied into the outfalls, thence into the sea. For efficiency, constancy, and preparedness no other land drainage system equals it, except perhaps for Holland which is in a very similar situation to the English Fens. In the Middle Level stand the giant Fen guardians – a massive complex of four impressive turbines and powerful diesel and electric engines capable in full song of discharging more than 6,000,000 tonnes of water every twenty-hours of continuous running. The Middle Level main drain collects water from various other drains and is linked indirectly to rivers in the Level, fed by dykes, water pumped along them by smaller units. This is impelled into the turbines and thrown out at the rear of the pumping station into the River Great Ouse. A large vehicle could fit easily into each snail-like turbine, among the largest in the world.

The Wiggenhall pumping units are linked to a highly sophisticated drainage system and it is fed by pumps of smaller capacities, water controlled by sluices strategically positioned in the Level. A powerful factor in the Fens' success in coping with excessive amounts of water, much of which originates from upland regions, are massive embankments towering above the rivers and arrow-straight drains. These give ample allowance for the water level to rise in unusually rainy seasons. In 2000 and 2001 when various parts of the country suffered disastrously from floods, the water level in the Fens did rise a few feet but there was never a threat of embankments being breached. The banks carry roads, another sensible feature in the Fens, and if the worse did happen and the fields became flooded, communication would still be possible between certain places. Elsewhere in the country recent floods made roads impassable and that added to the misery of those whose properties were inundated.

Serious drainage of the Fens began in the 17th century. In previous centuries spasmodic attempts were made to drain a few areas with little success but the experiments and mistakes proved valuable to successive engineers. Sir Cornelius Vermuyden, the renowned Dutch land drainage engineer, designed the first major plan including the construction of a major river, but it was none too successful. An extended plan involving a second river coursing parallel with the first for a length of about twenty miles, each river separated by a wide wash acting as a safety valve. It proved that the scheme to drain the Fens could work. From 1650 onwards with various improvements and a not inconsiderable amount of high technology, things began to make sense. For 350 years the Fenmen were engaged in all-out war against the elements and despite new methods and continuous improvement, flooding did occur from time to time.

It has been a costly experience. In the prolonged struggle over the years hundreds of lives were lost, properties ruined and destroyed and livestock drowned. Fen people learned their lessons from cruel, practical experience.

New rivers and dykes were cut for channelling water to no fewer than 800 wind engines which were useful when they worked, but often as not they were becalmed. New drains and a relief river were cut in recent years and these combine with the older drainage system which nowadays is reckoned to be capable of coping with severe wet weather for a prolonged time. The greatest risk will probably be measured if and when heavy snowfalls occur followed by a rapid thaw like that in 1947 when the system was overburdened and thousands of acres of fen land were flooded and properties and stock destroyed.

In that year, land around Haddenham and Ely was completely inundated and at Cowbit Wash and Crowland in Lincolnshire it was much the same story. Banks were breached and men worked feverishly night and day to plug them, even army tanks being used to temporarily close gaps. One of the ingenious methods used in keeping the Fens tolerably free of excessive water was the provision more than three hundred years ago of washland at Earith, Mepal and Welney, and at Whittlesey and Cowbit. These stretches of grazing grounds of extensive length and width serve as safety valves and are allowed to fill with water when occasion demands. In this way excessive pressure on river banks is relieved, the water eventually going back to the rivers and proceeding along respective channels to the outfalls. In the Fens washland is an artificial flood plain and there are no buildings

There are natural flood plains in many parts of Britain and seemingly innocuous rivers flow through them, the water line usually a few inches below the meadow. These natural rivers are unbanked and have no pumping stations along their length and few if any sluices to control the flow of water. It is conceivable that serious flooding of these areas had not occurred within living memory, perhaps for as long as a hundred and fifty years. Given the tendency for the country to receive more rain than usual it is surprising that local and county authorities give permission to build on plains which are now liable to flood. Acres of concrete foundations affect the natural soakway which is nature's way of dispersing water. We are realising that harmless looking and beautiful streams can become, like the tragic experience at Lynmouth, raging torrents and invasive water masses, a nightmare to those unfortunate enough to live near them.

The only logical way in attempting to confine water to natural courses is to embank the rivers. Like the Fen system it would probably work but such a precaution is unlikely to materialise on a dynamic scale, ruled out by

45

colossal expense of such an operation. In the Fens it has taken four hundred years of experiment to control the amount of water entering the area and systematically dispersing it using tides and a strategically planned highly sophisticated drainage system, quite the finest in the land. Most river banks in the Fens were thrown up centuries ago by voluntary and forced labour and these are maintained through the implementation of special drainage rates.

The inhabitants are well aware of the potential catastrophic disaster facing the Fens were it not for the sophisticated machinery and know-how born of experience. The drainage system is insurance in itself.

The wind may howl above the flat landscape and chill the bones. Green embankments rise reassuringly above the man-made drains and dykes, mile after mile, reflecting the incandescent beauty of the three-quarter sky and those inspiring sunsets for which the Fens are internationally renowned. Here and there an army of pumping units wait like crouching monsters for the inevitable rainy day.

We living in the Fens can be justly proud of our history, of the state-of-the-art drainage system born of centuries of struggle, disaster, poverty, loss and despair. Here in the nation's larder are profound lessons to be learned. If climatic change dictates the future in terms of natural disaster through persistent flooding of towns and the countryside, other low lying areas in the country may well have to observe and emulate the proved defensive system against potential inundation of the largest and lowest area of Britain – the Fens.

Floods surround a farm near Sutton-in-the-Isle.
(From the Cambridgeshire Collection with permission of Cambridgeshire Libraries)

Road cut off by floods near Mepal.
(From the Cambridgeshire Collection with permission of Cambridgeshire Libraries)

FLOODED FENS

ADDENDUM

Hundreds of years ago it was not unusual for large tracts of fen to be under water during the summer season. In 1285 Edward The First, crossing the Isle of Ely from King's Lynn, expressed his surprise that the floods were out in summer. When told that neglect to repair the banks along the lodes from the descent of fresh water from encompassing upland was the cause of inundation, he listened to complaints from the men of Wisbech and because of his royal dignity which bound him to protect the realm, directed his writ of enquiry to the Bishop of Ely who was invested with special powers, and others, to hold an inquisition to determine who was in default and how the problem could be speedily remedied.

From Ugg Mere near Ramsey to March and beyond to Wisbech the banks of the River Nene had been allowed to crumble apart. The "chares" (waterways) caused the trouble and allowed water to spread out into the marsh and this had affected other rivers in the region. Waters of the Ouse at Earith and at Littleport and of the Nene at Stanground and the Welland at Waldram Hall, having poured into the Fens from the surrounding upland and reaching a flat country had lost velocity and spread out from their normal courses. Gravity was almost non-existent so the volume of water had to mount over or pass under the water already in the channels. Therefore the Fens were continually subjected to incursion and build up of water which seriously affected outfalls and rivers, restricting their use. Much of the time they were filled with silt and this impeded the normal flow.

Remedial action involved the cutting of a straight channel from Littleport Chare to the Little Ouse and this relieved the Welney River. However, the affect upon the then natural system of drainage was not realised and the new work disturbed the river current which previously had had its main flow by Westwater to Benwick and then via the Nene at March, eventually discharging into the outfall at Wisbech.

In medieval times the Fen rivers were highways from the coastal region to upland towns. Supplies to Spalding, Stamford, Peterborough and Cambridge depended on water carriage via towns like March and Chatteris. Most Fen towns were minor ports and March, for instance, had a fleet of eight barges in the late 16th century. There were no proper roads in the Fens, except a few hazardous causeways which lay under water until the summer arrived and even then travellers came across unexpected difficulties. Fairs and markets in the Fens could only be supplied by vessels employed on the extensive river system. Traders relying on the area's waterways were frequently held up by too much water spilling into the rivers or not enough and, following complaints, the King sent a commission to look at the problem.

The division of the River Ouse from Westwater altered the volume from Benwick and the water tended to flow towards Earith with disastrous consequences for towns relying on the old River Nene. The men of Peterborough, Thorney, Whittlesey and March had to manage as best as they could until about 1478 when Bishop Morton had the new leam constructed to carry water directly to Guyhirn, thence to Wisbech and the Wash.

Well before the 17th century a system involving construction of embankments was introduced. It resulted in the raising of the river beds and it was soon realised that embankments required constant maintainance and added to the difficulties draining the low surrounding country. A number of inquisitions took place including one held in 1438:

"Inquisition held at Wisbech in the county of Cambridge . . . directed by King Henry the Sixth to supervise all banks, dikes and drains, sewers, bridges, causeways and gates by the sea coast and in the Fens . . . The jury say that the sea bank beginning at Tydd St. Giles as far as Bevys Cross in Wisbech ought to be kept at fifteen feet high and six feet wide at the top, and that every tenant of lands or tenements in the town of Wisbech and in the towns of Leverington, Tydd St. Giles and Newton according to the proportions of their holdings have been accustomed time out of mind to repair, sustain and make the said bank by reason of the said custom . . . each tenant is bound".

According to this, the tenants of Wisbech were under obligation to keep banks in good repair and "tenants at Townsheade and Fenbende repaired the marsh bank called Gebryncke on the north side from the great bridge at Wisbech as far as Soreldyke and Newdyke to Gehirn (Guyhirn), as far as

Piggesdrove Crosse taking into consideration the size of their respective holdings." Engines for drainage purposes along Wisbech bank were removed and anyone making dams or pools in the bank from Guyhirn to the sea which was then close to Wisbech was liable to suffer a fine of five shillings which would be given to the Bishop of Ely. A keeper was appointed to supervise the protection of the country and open and close the four gotes (gates) at Wisbech, Leverington, Newton and Tydd St. Giles. In addition it was decreed that the dyke called Elm Fendyke should be raised three feet higher. Redmoredyke in Elm which began its course at Coldham Clowse and extended as far as Friday Bridge was customarily "repaired and sustained" by all tenants of lands in the vicinity, and it was ordered to be raised four feet and made eight feet wide at the top. These repairs and alterations indicate that water was getting onto the land and could only be restricted to its course by making embankments higher.

WIND ENGINES NOT USUALLY RELIABLE

About eight hundred wind engines were constructed to assist in the movement of water through the labyrinth of drains towards the outfalls. Often they were becalmed when they were needed and storms and powerful winds wreaked havoc to the towers and canvas sails. It was not unknown for engines to cause floods rather than diminish the prospects of it happening. The largest wind engines were the double-lift type which received water from the smaller ones and lifted it to higher levels. Whittlesey parish alone had fifty wind engines and Manea parish was served by no fewer than thirty-seven. The village suffered considerably through regular deluges and several of the so-called protective engines actually threw water upon the parish. A tunnel excavated beneath the Old Bedford river in 1712 was supposed to discharge excessive amounts of water into the Sixteen Foot, originally named Thurlow's Drain. After excessive rain the tunnel was unable to cope with the increased volume of water which spilled into Manea.

The earliest wind engine in the Fens was erected at Elm by a Dutchman in the late 16th century. Earlier in that century horse mills were used to drain tracts of fen. The old Fenmen wrote of them as "grinding water", not corn! The horse mills seem to have been capable of ridding smaller areas of water in a relatively short time. Wind engines were set upon timber piles driven into a bed of clay and most had four sails. One mentioned by Daniel Defoe had twelve. Some scoop wheels had a diameter of twenty-five feet but farmers regarded them as a nuisance, the engines' efforts neutralised by the main drains which had insufficient gradient. As a result the water moved sluggishly and in times of heavy rain it built up and brought pressure upon the banks, sometimes threatening to create gaps and cause flooding. A hundred-and-twenty wind engines were used in the Bedford Level and all were pulled down between 1700 and 1716 because they did more harm than good. They were expensive to maintain and presented serious technical problems. Only two were allocated to the Norfolk Marshland and these provoked heavy criticism. It was suggested that at least thirty-two would be needed to make any difference to the area and that heavy expense would be incurred as compared with that of maintaining a natural drain, estimated at half. The wind engine at Tydd St. Giles was a good example of inefficiency, having to cope with two thousand four hundred acres; land owners had to erect another engine to assist it. This was the argument put forward in the matter of providing two wind engines for the Norfolk Marshland which land owners viewed with some amusement as the machines would have to struggle with draining about 40,000 acres.

By 1763 it was confidently expected that a considerable amount of drained fen would become increasingly productive. This was not always realised. At Cottenham, for instance, cattle let loose on supposedly dry pastures were "up to their bellies in water". Haddenham farmers, too, were exasperated in efforts to make land more profitable, as their acreages in the fen had been repeatedly inundated for fifteen years. They were unable to work the land and could not raise sufficient money to pay the rent. At times low lying land between Cambridge and Ely, despite intensive drainage work, resembled a lake and farmers had every reason to be distressed. Owners of land around Ely frequently observed water spreading over their fields and that prevented work with serious financial loss. In 1777 at Burnt Fen the bank gave way and practically every land proprietor was ruined. Sixteen thousand acres had to be given up by farmers and abandoned wind engines, unable to cope, testified for many years to the ruination of the area. Farmers were thrust upon parish relief in order to support their families with bare necessities. At Ramsey water regained in excess of 10,000 acres and workers were forced from their homes. The general opinion was that drainage by wind engines was imperfect and many proprietors said they were a waste of money. The keepers and their families moved into the creaking structures in October and prepared the engines for winter. A keeper's main responsibility was to maintain the mechanical parts and move the engine's head into the breeze and should gales threaten, to furl up the sails. During the summer he usually worked as a roder, cleaning out ditches.

50

Morton's Leam created by Bishop Morton of Ely in about 1478. Viewed from near the Dog-and-a-Doublet sluice, Whittlesey, the leam was not as successful as was hoped, being insufficiently wide and deep and unlike most existing rivers in the Fens, unbanked.

Beginning at Guyhirn the leam cuts through wash land and ends at Stanground. It was known to overflow onto adjacent land and the water spread out, adversely affecting other waterways including the old course of the River Nene at March.

(PHOTO: A. J. BALL)

OLD AND NEW BEDFORD RIVERS

Sir Cornelius Vermuyden's grand design to disperse water by confining it in an orderly fashion to numerous dykes and drains was highlighted in the cutting of the Old Bedford river from Salters Lode to Earith, a distance of 21 miles. There was much controversy from local people who, not without some justification, visualised the plan as being injurious to their livelihood as fishermen and wildfowlers. The Fenmen would not lift a finger to help with the scheme and it was left for large numbers of foreigners, drafted to the Fens, to dig drains and dykes, build sluices and erect wind engines. The labourers, some Huguenots and Walloons, had immense experience of land drainage effectively carried out in their own countries in Europe. They had also successfully drained Hatfield Chase, near Doncaster, but were forced to flee to the Cambridgeshire Fens by vexed Hatfield inhabitants, fearful of having their livelihood destroyed. Welcomed by the Earl of Bedford they exerted themselves in draining various parts near Whittlesey and Thorney and set their hands to schemes in various other areas of the Fens.

Opposition was rife but not as concerted as had been experienced at Hatfield. In May 1637 formal complaint was made to the Justices of the Peace to suppress the tenants and orders made that anyone guilty of inciting disorder and creating damage to the drainage works would be bound over and in the most serious cases, imprisoned. The Old Bedford river excavated in about 1630 did not fulfil expectations and in summer the land which it was supposed to have drained and made profitable was anything but that and farmers were doomed to disappointment. It was hoped to reclaim the whole of the Bedford Level and turn cattle onto the former flood plain for winter pasture. Vermuyden acknowledged that the land would not yield profit and accepted that inundation on a lesser scale than previously might be expected. Twenty years later the New Bedford river was devised to run parallel with the Old Bedford river and washland provided between the two waterways to take excessive amounts of water. To create the new river it was necessary for hundreds of Dutch and Scottish prisoners-of-war to be brought to the Fens, some stationed at Earith and others at Salters Lode, the two groups working towards each other. The Scots had been defeated by Oliver Cromwell at the Battle of Dunbar and the Dutch prisoners captured after a dramatic battle on the high seas.

(Read *"The River Makers"* and *"Water, Water Everywhere"* by the author, telling the story of Fen drainage).

FEN DRAINAGE ENGINES IN THE 16th CENTURY

A wind engine was installed in the marsh at Holbeach in 1587. This was said to be the earliest drainage engine in the Fens, but one was erected at Elm about the same year. By 1748 there were no less than 250 wind engines standing in the Middle Level of the former Isle of Ely. These were eventually pulled down and replaced by a much smaller number of steam powered pumps of the beam engine type, the first a 30 horse power machine installed at Ten Mile Bank in 1820. Ten years later 25,000 acres of land was being drained by two beam engines whereas prior to the advent of steam power it would have required seventy-five wind engines to drain the same area. They were suitable in certain conditions but in calm weather they could not work. Only seven wind engines were employed in the Fens in 1925; seven were derelict and the basements of two converted into residences. A wind engine at Christchurch and another at Soham were taken down and transported elsewhere and rebuilt again to serve as corn mills.

The vast majority of "windmills" in the Isle of Ely had been built to serve the drainage scheme but others were used solely to grind corn. Unlike several in Holland the Fens' wind engines never served the dual purpose of lifting water and grinding corn. The engines made sufficient progress possible in the late 17th and throughout the 18th centuries and some land was adequately dry and produced remarkable crops of oats, wheat, flax and coleseed on ground previously inundated. Some areas of fen were capable of producing two crops of wheat in a single growing season and women and young children were employed to deliberately trample the young wheat shoots into the ground to delay growth. Hemp, peas and onions appeared in the Fens for the first time and land which had been inundated for hundreds of years was so virile "it grew weeds on the banks almost as high as a man and horse". The rivers were given new energy as more and more farmers made use of boats and barges, and Wisbech and Ely markets benefited hugely from the Fens' new agricultural age. It was necessary to inaugurate a new market in the area and in 1669 one was set up at March to cope with the great amounts of produce being grown in the former Isle of Ely.

A TRAVELLER'S OBSERVATION OF THE FENS

Daniel Defoe recorded in 1724: "They (travellers) pass over here from Lynn into the Fen country and over the famous marshes into Lincolnshire. But the passage is very dangerous and uneasy, and where passengers often miscarry and are lost. But then it is usually on their venturing at improper times and without the guides which if they would be persuaded not to do so, they would very rarely fail of going and coming (back) safe".

Of decoys: "There are more of these about Peterborough who send fowl up twice a week in wagon loads at a time, whose wagons before the late Act of Parliament to regulate carriers, I have seen drawn by ten or twelve horses apiece; they were laden so heavy".

Of the Fen environment: "As these fens appear covered with water, so I observed too, that they generally at this latter part of the year appear also covered with fogs, so that when the downs and higher grounds of the adjacent county were gilden with the beams of the sun, the Isle of Ely looked as if wrapped up in blankets and nothing could be seen but now and then the lantern or cupola of Ely Minster. One could hardly see this from the hills and not pity many thousands of families that were bound to be confined to those fogs, and had no other breath to draw than what must be mixed with those vapours and that steam which so universally overspreads the (Fen) country. But notwithstanding this the people, especially those used to it, live unconcerned and as healthy as other folk except now and then an ague, which they make light of, and there are great numbers of very ancient people among them".

DROWNED LANDS AT MANEA

Manea suffered very considerably from inundation, many of the wind engines in the vicinity throwing water onto the parish rather than the reverse. The inhabitants were drawn into a very low state of existence from keeping between two and three thousand sheep to being quite unable to winter hardly three hundred. From some of the worst lands in the parish in about 1830, producing with little difficulty about sixteen combs of oats per acre, the land at Manea became impossible to plough at all. Awful poverty descended upon the parish and from being called ""rich Manea" as old time tradesmen from Ely called it in 1708, it was regarded as the poorest in the level.